THE

STORY

A Short History

Carl Chinn

Brewin Books

First published August 1998 by
Brewin Books Ltd, Studley, Warwickshire B80 7LG.

ISBN 1 85858 105 2
A British Library Cataloguing in Publication Data
Catalogue record for this book is available from
The British Library

Typeset in Caxton Book
made and printed in Great Britain
by Heron Press, Kings Norton, Birmingham B38 9TS

ACKNOWLEDGEMENTS

No author can write a book without the help, interest and goodwill of others. In particular I should like to acknowledge the generous support of Sir Adrian Cadbury, not only for reading drafts of my chapters but also for carrying on the tradition of the Cadbury family by striving for the well-being of Birmingham. I thank also the following who have given me advice: Charles Gillett, a former managing director of Cadbury Ltd; John Harvey, a former marketing director of Cadbury Ltd; Graham Parker, a former head of the design studio Cadbury Ltd; Richard Frost, head of public relations Cadbury Ltd; and Alan Palmer, former Cadbury Ltd marketing director. My appreciation goes to Sarah Foden Information Manager, Janet Harrison Library Administrator, and Caroline Wakeling in the Library for finding books and doing much photocopying of articles; and to Ken Taylor former archivist at Cadbury World, for invaluable assistance with my photographic research. Finally I thank a number of other of people for their contribution to making this book possible: John Henson, General Manager at Cadbury World; Tony Lass, Head of Agriculture, at Cadbury; Pauline Weaver, Public Relations Manager at Cadbury World; Richard London and his team at the Cadbury Schweppes Design Studio, for their help in finding illustrative material; and Alan Brewin, the publisher. I also wish to acknowledge the importance of the editors of the Bournville Works Magazine. The first-hand evidence which is to be found in this publication is remarkable. The BWM began in 1902 with J. H. Whitehouse and Clarkson Booth. Three years later T. B. Rogers became its first full-time editor. He retired in 1936 and was replaced by W. E. Cossons. His departure in 1955 led to the final editorship of Tom Insull. The BWM was replaced in 1969 by the Bournville Reporter whose editor was Harry Witcherley. The work of these men cannot be underestimated. They have provided an invaluable insight into the firm of Cadbury and the people associated with it.

THE CADBURY STORY:

I was very pleased to be asked to write a foreword to Dr Carl Chinn's lively history of the Cadbury business, which I have thoroughly enjoyed reading.

This is no dry account of the growth of an enterprise. It is written in Carl Chinn's inimitable style and is inspired by his enthusiasm for Birmingham and for the industry and commerce which lie at the City's heart. He brings the record to life by drawing on the personal reminiscences of those who worked for the Firm over the years.

This in turn is a reminder that family firms are made up not only of the family whose name they bear, but of all the other families who over the generations help to build such companies. The family spirit of the Firm comes through clearly in the narrative and is undoubtedly one of its strengths.

The interesting question is why the Firm of Cadbury should have emerged as the industry leader, when there were so many competing companies with similar origins? I believe that some of the answers can be found in Carl Chinn's book. The Firm remained true to certain principles from the very beginning and they have continued to stand it in good stead to this day. They include a strict regard for integrity in all the company's dealings, a belief in participation - that everyone counts and that all can contribute to the success of a business - and a commitment to quality and value. The Firm has never allowed itself to forget that its success depends on repeat purchases by literally millions of customers.

An early statement of the Firm's aims said it all:

"Our policy for the future as in the past will be: first, the best possible quality - nothing is too good for the public."

It was through standing by the principles of its founders that the Cadbury enterprise progressed from a grocer's shop in Bull Street to the international business of today.

That is the tale which Carl Chinn tells so eloquently in these pages. I am sure that you will share my enjoyment of it.

17th July 1998

Sir Adrian Cadbury

CONTENTS

Chapter 1: *Absolutely Pure. Therefore Best, 1824-79*

It was the most striking shop in Birmingham's most prestigious shopping thoroughfare. No other building had a window like that of number 92, Bull Street. Unlike the badly-made, green-ribbed windows of the other retailers it was made up completely of small squares of costly plate glass set in polished mahogany frames. The impression was clear: this was a forward-looking business with high standards of service and quality products. The shopkeeper himself was as impressive as his premises. Slim, precise and upright as a dart, he commanded attention both by his bearing and his speech. Strong of character and sometimes obstinate, yet he was kind, caring and courteous. His name was Richard Tapper Cadbury - draper, silk mercer and man of consequence.

He had come to the town in 1794. It was a turbulent and exhilarating time. The world was on the cusp of remarkable change. On the continent, the French Revolutionary armies were battling to spread the ideas of liberalism against the forces of the *ancien régime*. No longer were men and women prepared to be ruled by absolute monarchs. Now they strove for the triumph of the democratic will. Such a startling political transformation was matched by extraordinary social and economic shifts in Britain. Industrialisation was sweeping the land and as it did so country folk poured into the great manufacturing towns and cities of the Midlands and North of England, South Wales and Clydeside in Scotland.

Birmingham was in the vanguard of this switch from a rural, agricultural society to one which was urban and industrial. Acclaimed as the 'toyshop of Europe' the town's fame had been gained by men and women who took metal and forged and fashioned it into things of beauty. Buttons, pins, guns, buckles, coins, silver, gold, jewellery and a multitude of other goods were stamped, pressed, hammered and drawn in a host of local workshops. Commentators were amazed at the manufacturing prowess of the people of Birmingham, so much so that in 1784 a French writer called Faujas de Saint Fond declared that they had 'the genius of invention'. It was well-justified praise. Amongst the internationally-acclaimed Birmingham manufacturers were Henry Clay, who patented the making of *papier-mâché*, and John Baskerville. He designed an incomparable form of type and using his own presses and paper he printed editions of the classics which astonished the librarians of Europe. There were many other local 'heroes of the workshop' but chief amongst them was Matthew Boulton.

His ingenuity was renowned and by the late 1700s his factory in Handsworth was the largest in the world. It drew in enthusiastic foreign visitors and to the markets of the globe it sent out gilded bronze, silver plate and a variety of small metal wares. Yet Boulton was more than a great industrialist. He was also a man who gave other craftsmen and inventors an opportunity. It was his support which allowed James Watt to further develop the steam engine. It was his employment which enabled William Murdock to work on the discovery of coal-gas lighting. And it was his inspiration which drew together at his Birmingham home a group of thinkers who formed the Lunar Society. They included the scientist and chemist Joseph Priestley, the botanist Erasmus Darwin and the manufacturer Josiah Wedgwood. Their collective impact on the emergence of the modern world was immense.

Birmingham was not only an exciting, expanding town. It was dynamic and free. There was no corporation to stifle entrepreneurship, no dominant trade guilds to hinder enterprise and in a period when the members of the Church of England were privileged, Birmingham was attractive to Non-Conformists because it was seen as a town where a member of any sect could get on. In particular the town had a small yet significant congregation of the Society of Friends, or Quakers as they were known popularly. As elsewhere and like other Non-Conformists, they were legally excluded from studying at Oxford and Cambridge Universities, from entering certain professions and from representing a constituency in the House of Commons. Discriminated against in so many spheres, many Dissenters successfully focused their talents and energies on business and commerce. In Birmingham their numbers included the Lloyds, who founded a bank in Dale End in 1765; the Pembertons, who were ironmongers; and the Galtons, who were active in gunmaking.

Born in Exeter in 1768, and from a long-established West Country family, Richard Tapper Cadbury was also a Quaker. When he was fourteen he left home to begin an apprenticeship as a draper, eventually finding a job in London. Keen on starting his own business, he was told by his friend Joseph Rutter that there was an opening in Birmingham. Early in 1794 the two young men visited the town, attended the Bull Street Meeting and talked with Charles Lloyd and other local Quakers. Soon after, Cadbury and Rutter rented 92, Bull Street and on 23 July a letter was sent from James Phillips of London to Matthew Boulton.

> I am taking the liberty to introduce to thy notice and patronage two young men lately settled in Birmingham, to whom thy countenance cannot fail of being singularly useful, their names are Cadbury and Rutter, and if I did not think them of more than common worth I should not venture on this step - I have, however, not the smallest doubt but they will do my recommendations credit, and that they will when well known be an acquisition to the town.
>
> (William A. Cadbury, Richard Tapper Cadbury, 1768-1860, Birmingham 1944, p. 7).

Phillips's confidence was well-founded. Although Rutter left the partnership after four years, Richard Tapper Cadbury maintained the custom of Birmingham's leading citizens and in 1812 and 1813 Matthew Boulton's son bought fabrics worth the large sum of £18 9s 11d. Yet Cadbury was more than a businessman: he was a respected and significant person who was involved deeply in public affairs. He was on the Street Commission, a major body until Birmingham gained an elected town council in

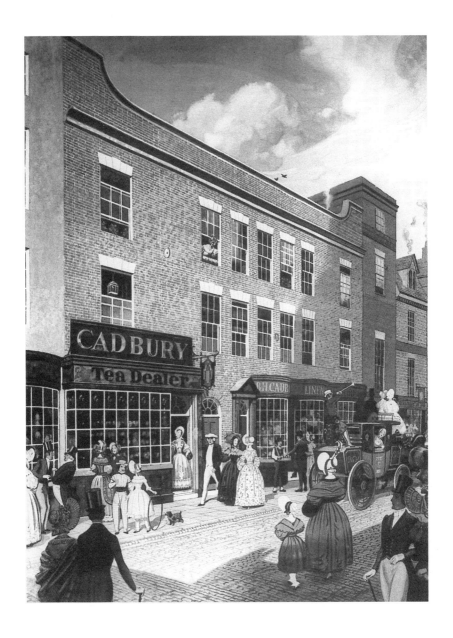

Bull Street in the 1820's from a drawing by E. Wallcousin (1824)

1838; he was an overseer of the poor; he served on the Boards of the General Hospital, the Dispensary, the Eye Hospital and other institutions; and he was active in promoting the railway line connecting Birmingham with Derby and Bristol. (*'Souvenirs of Richard Tapper Cadbury and Matthew Boulton', BWM, July 1950, p. 204*).

Richard Tapper Cadbury's importance was matched by that of his son, John. Born and raised in the living quarters above and behind the Bull Street shop, he left home when he was sixteen for an apprenticeship with a tea dealer in Leeds. He was a vigorous, alert young man and after he had served his time he moved to London, returning to Birmingham in 1824 when he borrowed money from his father to start a business. It was next door to his parent's, at 93, Bull Street. John Cadbury advertised that he would be opening for trade on 4 March, trusting that:

> *by assiduous attention to the interest of those who may favour him with their command, to merit their support, conscious that this can only be obtained by the sale of pure and genuine articles, which it will be his endeavour to sell them.*
>
> *Having had the advantage of residing a considerable time in a wholesale tea warehouse of the first eminence in London, and of examining the teas in the East India Company's warehouses and attending the sales, likewise of frequenting the Coffee-market, he is enabled to procure these articles equal to any house in the trade, and consequently can offer them on the most advantageous terms.*
>
> *He will regularly be furnished with Coffees of the finest quality, and a supply will be kept fresh roasted, which alone can insure a fine and delicate flavour.*
>
> *J. C. is desirous of introducing to particular notice Cocoa Nibs prepared by himself, an article affording a most nutritious beverage for breakfast.*
>
> *(Aris's Birmingham Gazette, 1 March 1824)*

Like his father, John Cadbury was determined that his business would be noted both for the excellence of its products and for the expertise of the proprietor. His emphasis on high-quality was crucial as many food retailers adulterated their goods with inferior additives. This was a practice which Cadbury eschewed. Impressed by his name, by his knowledge and by his wares, the noted families of Birmingham were attracted to his shop. The first customer was Samuel Galton, a fellow Quaker and well-known gunmaker who was also in the Lunar Society. He purchased 3lb of Souchong Tea costing 8s and 6lb of coffee priced at 3s 4d a lb. Other early patrons included the Boultons, Watts, Murdocks and Lloyds as well as the Rylands, the makers of plated and brass coach harnesses, and Kenricks, the hardware manufacturers.

In another move influenced by his father's approach to business, John Cadbury made sure that his shop window stood out. Not only was it made of plate glass but also it was filled with tea chests, caddies, cone-shaped sugar loaves and Chinese vases decorated with flowers and butterflies. Inside, attention was drawn by an effigy of a Chinese man. Dressed exotically and colourfully, he was placed by the long counter on which the tea

Richard Tapper Cadbury.

John Cadbury and his family. (1847)

The yard at the Bridge Street factory from an old bill-head.

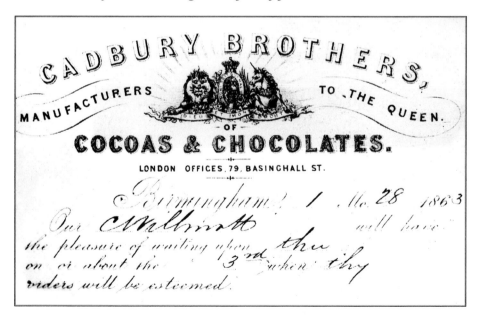

This advice card was sent out when the young Cadbury brothers, Richard and George, were struggling to put the business on a sound footing, and recover the trade which had dwindled. The factory was at Bridge Street, Birmingham. Note the Quaker phrasing and dating. (1863)

was gathered in a silver scoop and then weighed in brass scales suspended by lengthy chains. Besides the chests of tea there were bags of coffee beans, hops and mustard as well as packing cases. It was a fascinating shop in which tantalising smells roamed.

John Cadbury's trade was dominated by the sale of tea and coffee, but it is obvious that he was drawn to the marketing of cocoa. The sale of all three products were consistent with his staunch support of temperance and his desire to provide drinks which were an alternative to alcohol. Cocoa itself had originated with the Mayan people of Central America. They roasted and then ground cocoa beans to make a thick liquid to which they added water, maize meal, vanilla and chilli pepper. This bitter drink became popular with the Aztecs of Mexico and following their conquest by the Spanish the habit of chocolate drinking was taken to Europe. To make the taste less harsh and more sweet, the chilli pepper was left out and cinnamon, nutmeg and sugar were added. Chocolate drinking came to England in the mid-1600s, but was only taken up by the rich because of the high cost of cocoa. It was here that milk chocolate became popular, devised by the celebrated physician and botanist Sir Hans Sloane. The chocolate was sold in blocks comprised of squares, two to an ounce. To make a drink, each ounce was added to a pint of boiling milk with sugar to taste.

Despite its expense, by the late eighteenth century most towns had a shopkeeper who specialised in the sale of cocoa and drinking chocolate. As with the premises of John Cadbury, such tradesmen were to be found in the shopping streets favoured by the well-off. This was the case with Joseph Storrs Fry, a Quaker whose business was in Union Street, Bristol. Like other manufacturers he roasted the cocoa beans, sifted the kernels from the shells to produce the nibs, pounded the broken nibs and finally ground them. In 1795 Fry patented a new roasting process which was powered by a steam engine bought from Boulton and Watt, and by 1826 he was selling chocolate lozenges which were 'a pleasant and nutritious substitute for food when travelling'.

Although he had tried out his own processes by breaking up roasted cocoa beans with a pestle, John Cadbury did not become a manufacturer until 1831 when he rented a warehouse in Crooked Lane. Here 'he first experimented in the making of cocoa and chocolate' on a larger scale. Running from the bottom part of Bull Street, Crooked Lane was close to Cadbury's fashionable shop. The warehouse itself was four-stories high and had vaults below. It was a favourable time to make the leap from retailer to manufacturer selling to the trade. The consumption of cocoa nationally was increasing, from 122 tons in 1822 to 176 tons eight years later and to 910 tons by 1840. This growth was stimulated by a substantial reduction in the duty on cocoa in 1832, so allowing the sale of chocolates and cocoa powders 'at popular prices and for general use in England'.

('The Late John Cadbury', Birmingham Faces and Places, volume 2, Birmingham 1890, p. 22; W. A. Cadbury, 'Cocoa Cultivation and its relation to Bournville Trade and Prosperity', BWM, August 1936, p. 264).

*The Barron grinding mill used at the Bridge Street factory
and afterwards at Bournville. (1878)*

Little is known of the actual 'experiments' carried out by Cadbury although like all cocoa makers, he was faced with the problem of too much cocoa butter in his final product. The solution was to add potato starch and sago, so absorbing the butter and making the taste of the cocoa more palatable. More than most other manufacturers, however, Cadbury was intent on impressing the public with his high standards. In a business letter of 1841 he stressed the 'uniform quality' of his cocoas and chocolates. A price list from the next year indicates that he offered his customers sixteen types of drinking chocolate, including brands such as Broma, Churchman's Chocolate, Spanish Chocolate and Grenada Chocolate. Some were available in powder, others in cakes which buyers themselves ground or from which they scraped bits into a cup. Only one type, 'French Eating Chocolate', was not for drinking. Amongst Cadbury's eleven types of cocoa were Rock Cocoa, Granulated Cocoa and Soluble Cocoa - recommended 'as light and nutritious in its nature, grateful to the palate, and in price within the reach of all classes'. These cocoas were sold as powder, flakes, paste and nibs. John Cadbury's price lists emphasised that he rested 'his claim to the public support on his determination to maintain a character for a thoroughly good and uniform quality'.

(Iolo Williams, The Firm of Cadbury 1831-1931, London, 1931, pages 13-14;
T. B. Rogers, A Century of Progress, 1831-1931. Cadbury Bournville, Birmingham 1931, p12).

For all his growing involvement with cocoa and chocolate, wholesale sales of tea and coffee remained the mainstay of the business. This situation continued after 1847 when the Crooked Lane warehouses were knocked down to make way for the construction of a tunnel of the Great Western Railway. Forced out, Cadbury moved his business first to Cambridge Street and after a few months to premises in Bridge Street - across Broad Street from what is now Centenary Square. It had a warehouse, counting house, coach house and stable. The main building itself had two floors: on the ground were the storehouse, roasting ovens, kibbling mill and other machinery; and above was the packing room.

About this time John was joined as a partner by his older brother, Benjamin Head Cadbury, who recently had given up the drapery shop which he had taken over from their father. Two years later, the brothers pulled out of the retail side of their business and passed the Bull Street shop onto one of John's nephews, Richard Cadbury Barrow. That year, 1849, they showed 'Chocolate, Cocoa and Chicory in various stages of manufacture' at the 'Exposition of Art and Manufactures' - held in the grounds of Bingley House, the home of the Lloyds and now the site of the International Convention Centre. The display was eye-catching and it is likely that it was noticed by Prince Albert who attended the exhibition.

Cadbury Brothers had a growing reputation and in 1852 the Bridge Street factory and warehouses were visited by a London journalist, Walter White. He was impressed both by the location of the premises and the lack of smoke coming from the chimneys - achieved because of John Cadbury's keen support for smoke abatement. White then described the processes involved in the making of chocolate.

The only cocoa beans used were those from Trinidad and Grenada in the Caribbean. One hundred weight at a time they were roasted in one of four cylindrical ovens which span slowly over a coke fire. After that, the husks were removed in a kibbling mill and the nibs were placed in double cylinders. Each was warmed by steam and had within it a rotating length of iron. The heat and pressure combined to free the cocoa oil into a thick, slab-like substance which flowed into a pan and was ground between millstones. Heated once again it became a more loose liquid. This was poured into another pan and mixed with arrowroot, sago and refined sugar - in a clear distinction to some manufacturers who used cheap additives such as red earth or a pigment called umber. Next the mixture was issued into moulds where it solidified into cakes or blocks which were cut into shavings by a wheel wielding four sharp blades. Lastly, these flakes were collected and passed through a sieve to make them into a powder and prepare them for weighing and packing.

(*'Visit to a Chocolate Manufactory', Chamber's Edinburgh Journal, 30 October 1852*).

The high standing of Cadbury Brothers was made clear in 1854 when the firm opened an office in London and received the Royal Appointment as Cocoa Manufacturers to Queen Victoria. This accolade came in a difficult period. Although the government of William Gladstone had reduced further the duty on imported cocoa beans, the sales of cocoa and chocolate had fallen away during 'the Hungry Forties' and had stagnated during the 1850s. These economic problems were made worse for John Cadbury by the loss of his wife and a long-drawn-out illness. In 1861 he followed his brother Benjamin and stepped down from the firm, although in his broad-rimmed hat and white choker he continued to walk through the factory most mornings .

Starting work in 1866, Frances Stanley labelled packets before moving on to essence packing. She thought of John Cadbury as 'an old friend', a man who was kind to all those who knew him. His compassion was as evident in his public life. He was an active governor of the General Hospital and 'took a special interest in watching the surgical operations at that institution with a view to preventing any unnecessary cruelty being exercised upon the patients of the poorer class, an opinion at that time prevailing that the poor were operated on for the sake of medical science'. Numerous other organisations captured his concern and commitment, including the Society for the Relief of Infirm and Aged Women, the Homeopathic Hospital and the Blind Asylum; whilst he was a strenuous campaigner against the use of climbing boys to sweep chimneys.

(*Memories of Bridge Street and Early Bournville', BWM, October 1909, p. 366; 'The Late John Cadbury', in, Birmingham Faces and Places , volume 2, Birmingham 1890, pages 22-4*).

With John Cadbury's retirement his concern was taken on by two of his sons:

Richard Cadbury at the age of 26.
(1861)

George Cadbury at the age of 22. (1861)

Richard, who had entered the company at the age of fifteen in 1850; and George, who had begun work six years later when he was seventeen. Mary Grigg, another Bridge Street worker, brought to mind that 'Mr Richard was always smiling', whilst 'we thought that Mr George was stern, but he was very just'. H. E. Johnson was head of the firm's offices for thirty years from 1881 and he described the roles taken by the brothers. Richard Cadbury 'gave most of his time to the Sales side, whilst George Cadbury did the same for the Buying and Manufacturing sides, but they consulted each other so much that no definite line seems to have existed'.

(BWM, November 1950, p. 339; 'Centenary of the Birth of Richard Cadbury', BWM, August 1935, p. 279).

The brothers were hard-pressed to survive in the early years of their partnership. As George recalled in 1913:

The business was rapidly vanishing. Only eleven girls were employed. The consumption of raw cocoa was so small that what we now have on the premises would have lasted about 300 years. It would have been far easier to start a new business than to pull up a decayed one, but we were young and full of energy.

Each brother had been left the great amount of £4,000 by their mother, and they put the combined sum into the concern. Five years later Richard's share had dwindled to £150 whilst George, as he was not married, had £1,500. The situation looked so bleak that the brothers decided that if matters deteriorated they would close up whilst they were still able to pay their creditors in full. They had five depressing years, but after each time they took stock and 'we went back again to our work with renewed vigour'.

(Speech of George Cadbury, January 1913, cited in Rogers, A Century of Progress, 21 and 24).

The two of them were supported strongly by their workers. Tom King was a kibbler and he recalled that on the shop floor the hours were 'six o'clock in the morning till five in the evening, with half-hour breakfast and one and a quarter hours dinner'. The office staff laboured as strenuously. George Truman was appointed in 1862 as the firm's first clerk and like the brothers he put in a thirteen hour day, six days a week. Outside the factory, sales depended upon travellers who covered great areas and visited the maximum number of shopkeepers. Distinctive in his top hat and Scotch tweed coat, Dixon Hadaway was Cadbury's first such salesman and except for a few large towns he covered a huge area of Britain - from the north of Scotland to Northampton. Like his successors he journeyed by train, pony and trap or on foot and was often accompanied by a porter pushing a hand cart laden with samples.

('Memories of Bridge Street and Early Bournville', BWM, September 1909, pages 328, 338 and 340).

Gradually the brothers turned the business around. They dropped customers who were bad payers. They introduced new products such as Iceland Moss, a blend of cocoa and lichen which was marketed as a health product; and 'Chocolat du Mexique', a vanilla flavoured cake chocolate. And they paid great attention to the

Dixon Hadaway, the firm's first traveller, whose ground extended from Inverness to Rugby.

need to sell their products. From 1862 John Clark was the company's representative in London and the next year he received a letter from Richard Cadbury.

There is one point in thy letter we wish to touch upon and that is the working of the London ground and suburbs. We do particularly wish this well worked, as we believe it will ultimately repay both us and thyself to do so, and thou may depend if thou dost thoroughly work it we will see nothing is lost to thee whether with or without success. We will draw up a draft agreement without delay and forward it to thee to look over and make any suggestions thou wishes to. It is important for us both to pull together for we have much to do to conquer reserve and prejudice, and thou may be assured we will do our part in this in the way of improvement in style and quality of our goods. (Letter of 29 October 1862, in, 'The Battle of Bridge Street. A Centenary Retrospect', BWM, October 1947, p. 209).

Despite the precarious state of their affairs, the Cadburys were determined to be good employers. They started a Sick Club and at the end of the first year of its existence they gave the members a tea party - the beginning of the annual gathering. Mary Brown later became head forewoman at Bournville and she recalled that when George Cadbury joined the firm he began to pay female workers by the piece (how much they turned out). This trebled their previous wages of between 2s 6d and 7s 6d a week. Similarly, the brothers were amongst the first bosses in Birmingham to give their workers a 'half-day holiday' on a Saturday, and they were in the forefront of adopting bank holidays. Often when work was finished they would join in with the men in a game of cricket or football and each morning they held a reading in the stock room. For the clerk George Brice these religious services 'gave one the impression of being more like the early morning prayers of a family than a works meeting, and absentees were of rare occurrence'.

('Memories of Bridge Street and Early Bournville', BWM, September 1909, p. 329; 'Memories of Bridge Street and Early Bournville', BWM, October 1909, p. 362).

By 1864 the company had moved into profit and the brothers were keen to distinguish themselves from other cocoa and chocolate manufacturers. In particular, they sought a way to produce pure cocoa without the need for additives. George heard of a machine in Holland which was crucial to the making of fine cocoas. He went off 'without knowing a word of Dutch, saw the manufacturer, with whom I had to talk entirely by signs and a dictionary, and bought the machine. It was by prompt action such as this that my brother and I made our business'. The machine, a Van Houten Press, expelled some of the cocoa butter and did away with the need to add starchy ingredients. In 1866 the Cadburys launched their new unadulterated product in distinctive yellow packets. It was called Cocoa Essence.

(A. G. Gardiner, Life of George Cadbury, London, 1929, p. 29).

Writers in *The Lancet* and other medical journals praised Cocoa Essence. Such backing was crucial given that many mixed cocoas were promoted because of their value to personal health. Customers were gained by a vigorous advertising campaign.

Cocoa Advertisement. (1892)

In newspapers and journals whole pages were taken out and filled with favourable comments about the beneficial effects of the new product. A simple yet memorable slogan was adopted for use in such advertisements as well as on shop fronts and on the sides of horse-drawn omnibuses. It proclaimed that Cadbury's Cocoa Essence was 'Absolutely Pure: Therefore Best'.

The new line caused consternation amongst the other manufacturers of cocoa, many of whom decried the idea of a pure product. But Cadbury were in tune with the political and public mood. There were mounting worries about adulteration, so much so that one regulatory act was passed in 1860 followed by more stringent legislation in 1875. This swing towards wanting purity in food was acknowledged by Fry, the leading cocoa and chocolate maker in the land, when it soon followed the lead of Cadbury and brought out a product similar to Cocoa Essence.

The new pressing machinery gave another impetus to the growth of Cadbury. Cocoa butter is the essential ingredient in the making of eating chocolate. Mixed with sugar and added back into cocoa liquor, it allows chocolate to be set easily into moulds from which bars of chocolate emerge. With the cocoa butter that was left over there was an opportunity for the production of new kinds of eating chocolate. Refined plain chocolate was made for moulding into bars, whilst fruit flavoured centres were covered with chocolate. Bertha Fackrell was one of the first people to make these cremes. Like the other women workers she changed into a clean hard-wearing linen frock to carry on her job.

Oh, the job we had to cool the work! There were small cupboards with ventilators round the room in which we placed the cremes as they were made, the only kinds being 1d and 1/2d Balls and 1/4d and 1/2d Swiss Cremes and ten to the ounce and fourteen to the ounce Cremes . . . Sometimes when the boxers came for the work it was not ready for use, owing to the imperfect conveniences for cooling at that time, and that would settle work for that day . . . I remember once we girls putting our work on to the window sill to cool when someone accidentally knocked the whole lot down into the yard below. ('Memories of Bridge Street and Early Bournville', BWM, October 1909, p. 367).

The slowly increasing trade in eating chocolate gave Richard Cadbury an opportunity to use his artistic talent. In 1869 he was responsible for the business becoming the first in the trade to put pictures instead of printed labels onto chocolate boxes. His designs highlighted youngsters and often he used his own children as models. Colour printed in sheets they were pasted on to 3d, 6d and 1s boxes and were sold with cremes ten to the ounce. Two of his early pictures were also featured on fancy boxes for the three-ounce size of chocolate cremes: 'on one is a pretty marine view - a juvenile on the beach about to test the sailing properties of a fully-rigged toy ship; on the other an exquisite picture of a mother and child'. One of the best-known pictures was of 'a blue-eyed maiden, some six summers old, neatly dressed in a muslin frock trimmed with lace, nursing a cat'. It was praised in *The Grocer* for its

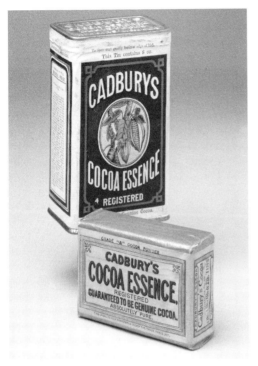

Early Cocoa Essence packs

Chocolate box designs by Richard Cadbury the inventor of chocolate box designs, taken from the Cadbury Family Book. (1870)

'artistic excellence'. Others were based on scenes noted by Richard Cadbury when he visited Switzerland.

(William Cadbury, 'Bournville and Art', BWM, March 1935, pages, 82-3).

There were less than fifty workers at Bridge Street in 1868 when David Jones was called to George Cadbury who 'put a sample case in my hand and told me to go where I liked for a week, the only stipulation being that I should not trespass on the ground of another traveller'. He introduced Cocoa Essence to North Wales and the borders, but found his greatest difficulty was 'the small demand for chocolate'. He gave hundreds of shopkeepers a taste of the product, 'only to watch their faces lose their customary shape, as if they had taken vinegar or woodworm'. Gradually retailers and their customers acquired a taste for eating chocolate, as they did for Cocoa Essence. The Christmas of 1873 was a watershed. The success of the new ventures led the brothers to abandon the tea and coffee trade along with the cocoas associated with additives. Only chocolate and 'pure cocoa being now made'. Jones became responsible for representing Cadbury's products in Lancashire. In his first year 'there was a great increase in the sale of Cocoa Essence, Mexican and other Chocolates'. The next year he doubled his turnover and in 1876 he was given an assistant, J. Penberthy. Within another twelve months business had grown so much that the district was split - with Jones taking the Manchester area and Penberthy that around Liverpool.

('Reminiscences of a Traveller', BWM, March 1904, pages 145-6 and 'Memories of Bridge Street and Early Bournville', BWM, September 1909, p. 336).

The expanding enterprise needed as much perseverance and involvement as had the struggling business. T. J. O'Brien began work at Bridge Street as a boy in 1869, beating creme by hand. On one occasion, the brothers came to help him. Tired out O'Brien left them to it - only to be rebuked. Later he and George Cadbury invented a machine to do this arduous job. He added that he 'never knew men work harder than our masters, who indeed were more like fathers to us. Sometimes they were working in the manufactory, then packing in the warehouse, then again all over the country getting orders.'

('Memories of Bridge Street and Early Bournville', BWM, September 1909, pages 329 and 340).

By the end of the 1870s Cadbury had grown so rapidly that it employed twenty-four office workers and travellers, 66 male workers and 140 who were women. The business had been transformed from the dire position of fifteen years previously. Innovation, artistry, hard work, clever marketing, strong support from its workers and above all quality products had propelled Cadbury into one of the biggest and best known chocolate and cocoa makers in the United Kingdom. Fry still retained its pre-eminence but Cadbury was poised to challenge the market leader. The means to do so were provided by a large, modern and well-equipped factory on a green field site.

Chapter 2: The Factory in a Garden, 1879-1899

The flourishing affairs of the Cadbury brothers presented a problem. Bridge Street was almost in the middle of Birmingham. The locality was packed densely with factories and workshops and it was hemmed in by a main road, side streets, a railway line and canal wharves and branches. There was no room for growth and yet the business desperately needed more space if it were to keep up with a waxing demand for its products. Faced with premises which were modest and inconvenient, it became apparent to the brothers that they needed to move. Accompanied by Henry Brewin and a few other representatives, each Saturday afternoon George Cadbury walked around Birmingham searching for a site for a new factory. At last he found a location which was large enough - fourteen and a half acres of land lying four miles to the west of the city in the agricultural district of Kings Norton. It was bought at an auction held by James and Lister Lea on Tuesday 18 June 1878.

Cadbury workers were equally aware of the commercial need for a new site. In the top creme room Bertha Fackrell and her fellows did their jobs 'cramped up' and it was a 'wonder that we turned out the work as well as we did'. Yet she was as alert to an altruistic motive for moving. She stressed that 'it was always the ardent desire of the heads of the Firm to take the workpeople out of the town, and to build "a factory in a garden" with plenty of ground for outdoor recreation'. The new estate would allow this aim to be fulfilled. Away from the industrial pollution of Birmingham it was a healthy spot surrounded by five farms: Lea House Farm stood close to the present Lea House Road, Stirchley; Two Gates Farm by the junction of Sycamore and Willow Roads; Bournbrook Farm by the cross-roads of Linden Road and Bournville Lane; Row Heath Farm at the meeting of Franklin Road and Oak Tree Lane; and Bournbrook Hall Farm later became the Girls' Recreation Grounds. Four of the named farms were owned by the Stock family, one of whose nurses is remembered in Mary Vale Road, Bournville.

('Memories of Bridge Street and Early Bournville', BWM, October 1909, p. 367).

The estate was a careful choice in other ways. It was large, it had scope for expansion and it boasted first-rate transport links. On its Eastern boundary were the Worcester and Birmingham Canal and the West Suburban Line of the Midland Railway. Opened recently in 1876 this locomotive route ran between Kings Norton and Granville Street, not far from the old building in Bridge Street. Fortunately the service had a stop at the village of Stirchley, or Strutley as it was known then, adjacent to the proposed factory. The other limits of the site were Bournville Lane to the south; what became Birdcage Walk to the west; and to the north a brook in which trout swam and which was called alternatively Merritt's, Griffin's or Bourn. It was decided to name the new premises Bournville, combining the one title of the stream with that of the French word for town. At this time eating chocolates from France were regarded as peerless and the Cadbury brothers wanted to place their firm on a par with the best.

(BWM, January 1924, p. 24; 'Correspondence', October 1931, p. 291; and 'From a Bournville Notebook', October 1953, p. 305).

In January 1879 work began on erecting Bournville. The brothers resolved not to go into debt and a rise in the price of cocoa made it even more important that costs were kept under control. To do this the firm acted as its own building contractor, employing construction workers and George H. Gadd as architect. Over two million bricks were laid under the supervision of the foreman bricklayer of Tangyes - the noted Quaker engineering firm in Smethwick. George Cadbury was deeply involved in the project. He helped to draw up the plans and oversee the construction. His son Edward was six and remembered that there were:

> great quantities of mud and thousands of bricks. A bonus was paid, I believe, at so much a thousand of the bricks laid, and the season was an unusually wet one. Another recollection was of going in the Bridge Street Works van from our house in Edgbaston to Bittel Farm at Barnt Green, where we stayed for some time when Bournville was in its early stages. The van no doubt carried my brother George's pram and cot. My father used to ride on horseback from Barnt Green along the lanes; there would be very few houses on the way; Cotteridge had not then been thought of.

('Remembrances of Things Past', BWM, December 1953, p. 381)

Like William Higgins of the creme tablet department, the workers 'looked forward to the time when we should actually be working in the midst of fields and gardens'. Excitedly they made 'many journeys to and fro to watch the progress', so eager were they to be at Bournville.

('Memories of Bridge Street and Early Bournville', BWM, page 365).

Construction finished in the autumn. The factory was a one-storey block facing Bournville Lane and its layout made plain the wide range of skills necessary for the mass production of quality products. There were a variety of sections associated directly with the primary objectives of making cocoa and chocolate. These included a girls' warehouse as well as rooms for storage, roasting, grinding, moulding, essence sieving, dressing and packing. But production required also a wide range of support staff, as was indicated by the saw mills; shops for tinmen, joiners and lathe operators; an engine house; and rooms for machinery, box-making, boilers and stoves. Then there were offices, stables, a coach house, a smithy and a sugar store. Lastly, space was provided for dressing rooms, a mess room, a kitchen, a dairy and reading rooms. Later when the factory was enlarged this whole block became the warehouse, stock room and export offices.

The move to these premises took a number of weeks. Much of the plant was carried by canal, which struck out from Bridge Street itself to the new factory. The

The original Bournville Works in 1879. In the foreground is a private road running parallel with the often muddy public lane. (1879)

A posed photograph of the packing department in the home warehouse, situated in a building near Bournville Lane, adjacent to the loading deck of those days, which was in front of the original 1879 factory. Timber was almost universally used for packing, in the form of cases, boxes and shavings. Note that much of the wood was printed, generally in red and black. Electric light had not yet been introduced: supplies were limited and costly. (1896)

*Caroline Jolliffe, born Alexander, started work at Bridge Street in October 1860,
She transferred to Bournville, leaving the company with a marriage gift
in October 1887. (1929)*

first person to begin work at Bournville itself was Arthur Koertgen, and he was soon joined by the office workers and those employed in the roasting department. W. France and his foreman Henry Sleath claimed the honour of making the first chocolates of the Travellers' brand.

('Memories of Bridge Street and Early Bournville', BWM, October 1909, p. 373).

Still, after a lay off of seven weeks, the main body of women workers did not clock on at the new factory until early in the autumn. On 27 September 1879 Richard Cadbury wrote to his father, John:

One more day is over, and now I have cleared out all my furniture from the old spot; table, books, and safe are all deposited in my new office. It is with some regret that we part with old associations bringing back past memories, but the world and time move on and we must move with them. I expect that the change will be very beneficial to us and to our workpeople. The mess room was opened last night for the first time for the girls' tea and it answered admirably. About 100 who stayed later than the others availed themselves of it. *(' From Bull Street to Bournville', BWM, September 1940, p. 202).*

Susan Floyd had been at Cadbury a year when the switch was made to Bournville. She lived in Waterloo Street in the centre of Birmingham and although the railway company had agreed to provide cheaper workmen's fares, the suburban train service did not begin until 8.30 in the morning. This caused problems when there were early starts in periods of peak production like Christmas. On these occasions Susan and other workers had to walk to Bournville and back home again. This meant waking at four in the morning and leaving an hour later so as to arrive at work for 6.00 a.m. Fanny Price brought to mind how some girls 'got lodgings in Stirchley' but as it was 'a very small village the large number of people could not find accommodation'. As a result the firm, 'who had just had the cottages adjoining the works built, temporarily furnished bedrooms and sitting rooms for the remainder of the girls'. Caroline Alexander was in charge of these operations. She had been with the firm since 1860, and it was she who 'bought bedsteads and blankets'.

('Mrs Grove Remembers Bridge Street', BWM, February 1954, p. 46; 'Obituary', BWM, February 1935, p. 57).

George Cadbury took a great interest in the welfare of the women. According to Fanny Price 'he came into a room at breakfast time to see we had a good meal', and later 'cooking classes were also arranged, and a lady engaged to give lessons to the girls'. At one stage, the company hired a van to bring other workers from town and at last it 'induced the Midland Railway to run an early morning train'. Bertha Fackrell shared those 'rough times'. Bournville Lane had no lamps so that 'in winter's time twos and threes would go arm in arm, groping their way along'. Yet 'we were very happy, for everything that thoughtful kindness could do for our comfort was done'.

('Memories of Bridge Street and Bournville', BWM, October 1909, pages 367 and 376-9).

As at Bridge Street, Richard and George Cadbury were involved in every aspect of the working life of the factory. H. E. Johnson was head of the offices and as he stressed, the brothers had literally made the business. They 'were acquainted with every detail' and regularly they could be seen testing cocoa beans, sugar and flavourings'. According to Richard's son, Barrow Cadbury, 'no two partners ever worked in more complete harmony'. There was a private passage between their offices and 'consultations were taking place continually'. Richard himself entered the weekly items of 'income and expenditure of the business in the balance books'; whilst Edward Cadbury praised his father, George, for his 'wonderful instinct for costing'. Until 1907, when a Cost Department was started, he kept detailed Cost Books in his own writing and in which he recorded prices for cocoa, sugar and other raw materials. Including expenditure on selling and advertising, he allowed 15% to cover all overheads.

(Rogers, A Century of Progress, p. 43; Percy W. Bartlett, Barrow Cadbury: A Memoir, London 1960, p. 36; and Edward Cadbury, 'Bournville in the Nineties', BWM, January 1935, p. 7).

The versatile talents of the brothers were complemented by the wide-ranging abilities of a number of employees. They included William Tallis. Orphaned at the age of nine, he joined the firm in 1862. Energetic and plucky, five years later he was made works foreman, a post he held until 1900. As Barrow Cadbury stressed, Tallis was ready to tackle anything - from engineering problems to sales visits to France and the USA. Mary Brown was another forceful and flexible worker. She began with Cadbury in 1858 as a girl and later was promoted to works forewoman. At Bridge Street she kept all the books relating both to the chocolate and the internal operations of the factory. She continued in her overseeing position at Bournville until 1903. Jemima Tattersall was another other crucial employee. Starting as a plain chocolate moulder in 1866, she rose to be head of the Stock Room before retiring in 1907. Then there was Tom King, a kibbler, whose family moved into one of the sixteen semi-detached houses built by the Cadburys for key personnel.

Shifting to the countryside was an extraordinary success. Fanny Price noticed that 'orders after a time came in so fast, however, that the rooms at length became overcrowded'. The firm took on young women who addressed envelopes for sampling cocoa by post. Many of them were from the nearby villages of Kings Norton, Stirchley, Northfield, Selly Oak and Bournbrook. Amongst the young men to start was E. J. Dalby. A 'man of high integrity' he became foreman of the Cocoa Sieving Department and stayed with Cadbury for over forty years. Within a short time, the number of employees had risen from 230 to 300. Ten years later the figure had swollen to 1,193, and by the end of the century it had reached 2,689.

('Memories of Bridge Street and Early Bournville', BWM, October 1909, p. 376; Retirements', BWM, September 1921, p. 228).

This huge expansion was propelled by a spectacular growth in the consumption of cocoa and chocolate in England. In the 1820s a mere 523,000 lb. of cocoa had been imported; by 1894 it was 22,440,000 lb. Because of its high national standing and

Works from railway station, about 1896.

This giant melangeur was for some years in the Chocolate Mill towards the end of the nineteenth century.

The arrival of the daily milk train was a feature at Bournville before the building of the milk factories. (1912)

The Marzipan Cutting Department in 'C' Block Top. Notice the gas lights hanging from the ceiling. (1900)

modern factory, Cadbury was assured of a major share in this enlargement. In that year the company sold 1,345 tons of Cocoa Essence, an increase of 200 tons over the previous year; and 3,427 tons of chocolate. Four years later the continued and impressive rise in cocoa imports drew comment from Sir M. Hicks Beach, the Chancellor of the Exchequer. In his budget statement he declared that cocoa was 'an admirable beverage' and 'not a little' of its increased consumption was due 'to the remarkable success of a certain well-advertised brand which, in gratitude to the maker, I am half-tempted to name'. There was no doubt that he referred to Cadbury, and the chancellor's comments were highlighted in the firm's subsequent adverts. *(Edward Cadbury, 'Bournville in the Nineties', BWM, January 1935, p. 7; 'A Chancellor's Praise for Cocoa', BWM, April 1954, p. 1).*

The pronounced upturn in trade meant that quickly the new premises themselves became inadequate for the company's requirements. Within seven years considerable extensions had been made, both upwards and outwards. They were followed soon by yet more additions. In 1895 the company bought the adjoining Bournbrook Hall estate, which allowed further developments and within four years the factory space was almost three times as great as that of the original works. Similarly, improvements were made in communications. In 1884 a siding was constructed linking the factory and the railway which had become a double track. Now part of the main line it connected Bournville directly not only with the central station in Birmingham but also with other major towns and cities.

Yet canals retained their significance for transportation and the essential cocoa beans themselves were brought in from Liverpool to a wharf kept by William Sparrey. Cadbury regularly used the carrying firm of Fellows, Morton and Clayton, by whom George Dale's father and mother were employed. They worked a pair of canal boats, a motor and butty, conveying cocoa and chocolate from Bournville to Sharpness on the Bristol Channel for the merchant ships to export. Later Cadbury was the first English company to use its own powered barges, all of which were decorated in the firm's livery.
(Letter to Carl Chinn, July 1997).

Within the factory, workers were turning out an increasing range of chocolates. In particular, the Cadburys were keen to challenge the supremacy of the French firms in the fancy chocolate market. Just one year after the opening of Bournville they appointed Frederic Kinchelman, a master confectioner, as their own head confectioner. Known as 'Frederick the Frenchman' he introduced lines such as Nougat-Dragées, Pistache, Pâte Duchesse and Avelines. These fancy chocolates were packed in ornate boxes and were even sold in miniature boxes, plush jewel boxes and silk-lined caskets with mirrors. Many of these boxes were designed by Miss Sophia Pumphrey, 'a gifted artist' who had been appointed in 1896. Similarly the drawing of advertising posters was the responsibility of H. N. Bradbear. After his 'untimely death' in 1917, Miss Lindsay became the chief art designer.
(William Cadbury, 'Bournville and Art', BWM, March 1953, p. 83).

By the end of the nineteenth century, Cadbury had a range of over 200 fancy boxes to offer retailers, some sold for as much as a guinea; whilst it produced nineteen lines of Easter egg. This product had been introduced in 1875. It was made with dark chocolate, had a smooth, plain surface and unlike the solid French-style eggs, it was filled with dragees such as sugar-coated almonds. The later eggs were more decorative and varied. Plush eggs were packed singly, were filled with chocolate and cost 3s 6d. This was at a time when the poverty line was set at an income of 20s a week for an average family. Plover eggs were the cheapest at 2d each.

('Remembrance of Things Past', BWM, December 1953, p. 3; 'Two Thousand Years of Easter eggs', BWM, March 1955, p. 73).

The travellers who sold the Cadbury products were essential to the continued success of the company. It was not an easy task. Barrow Cadbury was Richard's oldest son. Joining the business in 1882 he laboured in the 'hot room', packed boxes, ground cocoa so that he 'knew the smell of it' and sold goods from Sevenoaks to Southend. As with all Cadbury travellers, he sent an 'Advice Card' before he called on a customer, hoping 'to have the pleasure of' waiting on them 'when the favour of your orders will be esteemed'. Regular clients would write on the card the goods which they required, but new trade had to be gained in a more painstaking manner.

> *It was no sinecure carrying the heavy sample case - three or four samples of quarter pound Creme Cake (the real thing), and other chocolate and confectionery; very different from carrying photographs or aluminium dummies. I remember that after a hard day's work I was very thankful if I had collected as much as £40 to send home.*

Travellers were also responsible for encouraging retailers to advertise Cadbury products in their windows, above their front doors and alongside their premises.

(Bartlett, Barrow Cadbury, pages 33-4; Our Representative Hopes to Have the Pleasure', BWM, October 1967, p. 337).

After learning various aspects of the business, Barrow Cadbury concentrated on accounts and finance, signing all cheques over £40. Although he preferred to do things by hand, he introduced telephones, typewriters, loose-leaf ledgers, punched cards and accounting machines to Bournville. He also bought raw cocoa and vanilla at produce auctions in London and looked after advertising. The firm made effective use of its rural location. Increasingly advertisements featured the phrase 'The factory in a garden', often accompanied by sketches of the recreational facilities provided by the firm and of the works set amidst trees. The unusual location of the factory, its significance to the manufacture of chocolate and the Cadbury family's social conscience all combined to draw observers to Bournville. From 1881 the firm had kept a visitors' book and in 1902 a Department was set up under the supervision of Barrow Cadbury to look after these guests. So great was the interest in Cadbury that eight years later a film, 'A Day at Bournville', was produced.

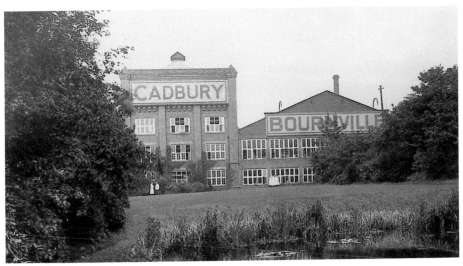

The stock building, despatch desk and ornamental pool in 1921.

Corner Shop in St. Saviours Road, Saltley, advertising Cadbury products, about 1890s (Thanks to Joe Molloy).

Increasingly, Cadbury was becoming an international concern. Since the 1870s, its products had been sold in Canada by Edward Lusher of Montreal and in Chile by the exporting firm of Messrs Brace, Laidlaw and Co. Towards the end of the decade, a shop was opened in Paris at 90, Fauborg St Honoré - more for the prestige that would be gained by having an address in the country famed for the quality of its chocolate. However, the opening of Bournville encouraged the development of the export trade. In 1881 Cadbury sent Thomas Elford Edwards to Melbourne to represent the company in the whole of Australia and New Zealand. Not surprisingly, a year later he was joined by an assistant, William Cooper. Another old Bridge Street worker, he was given charge of Queensland and New South Wales. Initially annual sales were the equivalent of those in the English town of Ashton-under-Lyne but business did improve - as it did in Canada and the USA. Consequently in 1888 an Export Department was set up at Bournville. Five years later a representative was sent to South Africa, whilst J.E. Davis was appointed to cover India, Burma, Ceylon and the Far East. Enthusiastic and energetic, he made sales in Gibraltar and Malta on the outward journey. So great was his influence in India that he became known as 'Cadbury Davis'.

('Selling the World', BWM, June 1948, pages 115-8).

The goods sold were made largely with traditional skills. Marzipan cutting, essence weighing, the running of creme into flour - all were done by hand. So was the crucial task of moulding chocolate. As described by A. J. Turner, as late as the early 1890s the only machinery involved in this process were four shakers, an air compressor, and a cooler. Chocolate was stoved from between a week to a fortnight at temperatures between 120° and 140° F. When it was ready for moulding it was 'the consistency of a thick paste'. Mexican chocolate, for example, was dug out of pans, put into the mixer and run down to a softer paste with the addition of a little cocoa butter. It was then put on to a wooden table where a large heap was made sufficient for a day's work. The butter in the chocolate permeated through the mass and approximately 50lbs of chocolate, a mix, was cut from the heap. This was taken over to wooden tables where it was tempered by kneading it so that slices could be cut from it and forced back into the middle for more kneading. When ready, the chocolate was laid out in long strips, cooled, gathered up and kneaded once more until the correct consistency and temperature for moulding was reached. The moulding itself took place on self-contained wooden tables. The air was heated by gas jet and when the chocolate reached the correct temperature it was cut into large slices and placed on the warm table.

Each moulding unit had a team of four youths and a boy led by a man. He kept the chocolate together by cutting off the large pieces lying away from the mix and forcing them into the middle to stop them becoming cold. With a large-bladed knife he also cut off the chocolate from the filled moulds. Each youth had six moulds. He took a large section of chocolate from the mix, rolled it into a long thin piece and laid it along a mould before forcing it in. The chocolate was smoothed off and the surplus removed. As for the boy, he picked up the moulds, placed them in an iron tray and passed them to a shaker who 'vigorously shook the moulds to break the air bubbles, and smoothed the chocolate again'. Lastly he used a toy banister brush to make the chocolate glossy. Lads with well-developed forearms were valued as shakers. Once moulded, the chocolate was put in a cooler 'which had an intermittent travel'. Arriving at the unloading end of the travel, the moulds were knocked out on to a paper and stored in wooden trays until needed for wrapping. This was done by hand as was the weighing of the chocolate.

('Chocolate Moulding', BWM, January 1937, p. 8).

Hand skills maintained their importance, but gradually more machinery was introduced into the factory. By 1887 the company had a pair of 25 horse power engines which drove a central flywheel; a single 25 h.p. engine; and a 40 h.p. engine which drove the saw mill. This section also had two Lancashire boilers, whilst there were three more in the main building. Much of the machinery was purchased from Tangye's, amongst it the cocoa mills and presses; but, like the 'Monster Mixer', some came from abroad. Between 1887 and 1900, the engineering side of the business was under the control of Richard Cadbury's second son, William. He had trained in Gloucester and then spent eight months in the machine shop and drawing office of the Stollwerck chocolate factory. After his appointment he continued to visit Germany and other English factories to gain ideas and was responsible for designing new plant such as the first steel kibbling machine.

His influence was evident elsewhere in the factory. In 1891 a new Card Cutting Department was opened. It was provided with one small and six large guillotines; two snip machines; three hand knives; two cutting out presses; three scoring machines; and three nicking machines. Together, they cost £1087. Three years later the value of the machinery had almost trebled and it now included nine power guillotines and five cornering machines. Elsewhere in the works were Avery machines for weighing essence, box-nailing machines and hand labelling machines for essence packets.

('William A. Cadbury, 1867-1957', BWM, August 1957, p. 271; and Edward Cadbury, 'Bournville in the Nineties', BWM, January 1935, p. 3)

The workers put in a 53½ hour week. This was long but less than in most other factories, whilst Cadbury was in the forefront of shortening the time spent at work. On 24 October 1898 the hours were reduced to 48, and in 1919 they dropped to 44 when Saturday ceased to be a full working day. There were firm rules concerning lateness, stealing, inferior work, wasting materials and the eating of chocolate. Those who broke these regulations could be fined or discharged, although those who kept them were rewarded. Fining for minor offences was abolished in 1898. It was replaced by the keeping of record cards which were considered periodically. From then on workers who infringed the rules could be cautioned, suspended or, rarely, sacked.

There were specific regulations relating to the employment of women. No man could enter a woman's department unless he wore a special arm band and no woman was employed 'who is not of good moral character'. Because of the insistence of George Cadbury, women had to leave their jobs when they married. This was an unusual order in Birmingham, where the work and skills of married women were essential to a large number of manufacturers. But like many other men of his background, George Cadbury did not want to 'take mothers away from their homes and children'. He felt also that employed married women had husbands who 'were quite content to loaf about doing nothing, living on the wages of their wives'. *(Gardiner, Life of George Cadbury, p. 31).*

From 1887 a marriage gift of a Bible and a carnation was given to the women who had to leave because of the firm's ruling. Mrs Payne was one of those who received it. She started at Bournville in 1897 and remembered vividly the stern forewoman.

I walked to the Works from Halesowen on the first morning - and I set out not knowing the way! But I was set on first time - and that was unusual. I can see little Mary Brown now. Dress down to the ground, her keys hanging from her belt. We new girls were lined up in a row and she walked up and down looking us over. And as she went she would say, 'You come forward . . . You come forward . . . You come forward . . . All you others go home. I only want so many this morning.

After a time on fondants without chocolate on, Mrs Payne went on to boxing and then essence weighing. She was on quarter pound tins, each of which was weighed by hand and 'the scales had to be absolutely level, not a fraction over or a fraction under'. Once a month 'there was a day, and you never knew which day, or the hour or the minute, when the forewoman would come round and take some of your tins for checking'. If one of the tins 'was a fraction under or over there was trouble!'
('Memories of Old Bournville', Bournville Reporter, May 1979, p.8).

In spite of such strictness Bournville was a popular place to work and older employees were enthusiastic for their young relatives to follow them into the company. Hilda Pratley's family highlighted this trend.

My father's mother, Mary Ann Timms nee Banner, worked for Cadbury's at Bridge Street before they moved to Bournville, so did her sisters, Anna, Helen and Susan Emma. Their brother Thomas Banner, too, who still worked in the printing when I went to work in Q Block, trainee hand box maker. My cousin Brian Banner worked in card cutting till joining the Air Force, World War II. My father also worked in moulding till 1927 . . . My cousin and I were the last members of the family to work for Cadbury's 1935-1944. (Letter to Carl Chinn, 25 July 1997).

Some families had even longer records of service. Edward S. Edwards started at Bournville in 1882, retiring twenty-nine years later. Before her marriage his daughter Emily was in labelling and her son, Leslie George Moreton, was employed for almost fifty years in Chocolate Block and Moulding. His daughter, Betty, had a job in the firm's Post Office and her son, Philip C. Sheward began service with Cadbury in 1965.
('More Service Records', BWM, January 1967).

The girls playground near no.1 lodge. (1890)

The Works' Orchestra, conductor Franklyn Restall. 1896

Bournville's attractions as a factory were clear. It was new and clean - and from 1897 many areas were lit by bright electricity instead of shimmering gas. It was set in countryside; the wages were good compared to most other manual jobs; and the company provided its workers with recreational facilities. From the opening of Bournville they had the use of a number of six foot by three foot gardens by the roasting mill. Nearby was a horizontal bar for those who wanted to do gymnastics. Boys and men played football and cricket in a field near the railway line; whilst just inside the works' entrance the girls and women sat or swung in a garden.

In 1895 the purchase of the Bournbrook Hall estate allowed the Cadburys to provide the men with a proper sports ground and the women with larger gardens. A year later a Men's Athletic Club was formed, followed in 1899 by a Girls' Athletic Club. By the outbreak of the First World War, female employees were involved in a variety of athletic activities such as cycling, tennis, cricket, hockey, netball and swimming - whilst girls of sixteen and under were required by the company to take part in gymnastic classes. A variety of other clubs and activities were encouraged by the company, such as the Musical Society. This embraced a brass band, which played in Bournville Village Park as well as in parks elsewhere in Birmingham; and an Orchestral Society led by its conductor, Franklyn Restall. He was Head of the Men's Wages Department and by 1919 he was one of only eighteen workers remaining who had been employed at Bridge Street. He retired the next year and the company 'had pleasure' on 'looking back on his co-operation in the anxious times when the foundations of the business were securely laid'.

('Memories of Bridge Street and Early Bournville', BWM, p. 380; and 'Forty Years of Works' games, BWM, July 1939, pages 214-20; 'Bournville Musical Society, BWM, September 1906, p.1).

From the opening of the factory, the employees had been provided with a kitchen in which to cook their dinners and in 1886 Cadbury became one of the first firms to open dining rooms with kitchens and the sale of food. Edward Cadbury mentioned that his father, George:

> *made a great point of providing fresh fruit at as low a price as possible, in order to encourage the habit of taking fruit. I remember, too, that we had to stop the sale of pickle and sauces, as the girls were in the habit of having a cup of tea, bread and butter, and some pickles and sauce, for their dinner, which we did not regard as at all a nourishing meal! Nowadays, of course, we are not so grandmotherly. ('Bournville in the 'Nineties', BWM, January 1935, p. 6)*

As was the practice in the factory, men and women had separate dining rooms. In 1895 and 1902 the Women's Dining Room was extended and a year later an organ was installed. This room was also used for the morning readings until they were discontinued in 1912 when the number of workers wishing to take part in the service became too great. In 1926 a new Dining Block was built and the old women's room became the Engineers' Office.

('The Life and Times of the First Girls' Dining Room', BWM, July 1956).

Richard and George Cadbury were paternalists. They had certain codes of conduct and they expected their workers to adhere to them. By today's standards they might be judged as men who interfered in the lives of others. By the standards of the day they were caring employers who felt that they were justified in pushing forward what they regarded as good ways of living. They were determined to get on and make money, but they were not selfish and stingy. They believed that they owed a responsibility to their workers and to the communities in which they lived. They carried out their duties by spending much of their time and money on the well-being of others. Both brothers were active in the Adult School Movement, voluntarily teaching others to read and write; both paid substantial sums for premises to further the aims of the movement; and both gave generously to other good causes.

Their children were imbued with this belief in service. Edward Cadbury explained that a business should be prosperous because without a profit 'we could not do the things we wanted to do'. An unsuccessful business was of no value to the community; it became a menace as 'the plant and buildings deteriorate and the workers have no security of employment'.

So it has been my aim and that of the other directors - and I don't think it is a low aim - to make the business profitable. My second aim has been to try to make Bournville a happy place. The provision of amenities, of good buildings, is of course a help, but a spirit of justice, of fellowship, of give-and-take, an atmosphere of cheerfulness, are more important than material surroundings . . . My - our - third aim has been to serve the community as a whole, by always giving the public a high standard of quality, at a reasonable price, striving to be efficient and enterprising in our policy. We have also tried to make Bournville an asset to the neighbourhood.
('Remembrance of Things Past, BWM, December 1953, p. 381

These were the principles upon which John Cadbury had founded his business in Bull Street. They were the principles adhered to by Richard and George Cadbury as they transformed their company into one of the leading cocoa and chocolate makers in the United Kingdom. Richard himself died in March 1899, whilst he was on a visit to Egypt. He was buried at Lodge Hill Cemetery in Selly Oak. A few weeks previously he and George had agreed that when one of them died then his executors and the surviving brother would convert the business into a private limited company. It would cease to be a personal concern. The terms of the agreement were carried out. On 13 June 1899 Cadbury Brothers Limited was incorporated. The capital was £950,000. George Cadbury became chairman of a board including Barrow, William, Edward and George Junior. It met first on 5 July 1899. One of its first duties was to receive the honour of the Royal Warrant, first given to John Cadbury in 1854.

Early girls' dining room. (1886)

"The Coach", a drawing by Cecil Aldin. (1899)

Chapter 3: Cadbury's Dairy Milk, 1899-1918

Although he had died in 1889, John Cadbury had lived to see his business become one of the most important in Birmingham. Ten years later, it was one of the most significant in England. Richard and George Cadbury had been spectacularly successful. Their business was a market leader in the United Kingdom and its products were sold around the world. They employed 2,685 people and the floor area of their works was seven times greater than it had been in 1879. This was a powerful base from which the new firm of Cadbury Brothers Limited could launch itself into the twentieth century. Led by the formidable George Cadbury the directors of the new board were not complacent. They realised that their business had to continue to hold fast to the standards which had made it famous. It had to be forward thinking, well-organised, alert to changes in fashion and taste, original in its product range and committed to quality, value and fair dealing.

The new company remained family-owned, although in early 1912 it did become a public concern. Still there were immediate effects of the shift away from a personal affair to one run by associates. Most obvious were the weekly board meetings. These were described by Edward Cadbury 'as quite a revolution in the control of the business'. Radical change was as noticeable in the day-to-day running of the company. The board quickly recognised that specialist sections needed to have their own identity within the broader Cadbury organisation. Each director was appointed to supervise a department. The first was Engineering, set up in 1900 under the remit of William Cadbury. It was headed by his cousin Louis Barrow and within two years the engineers were making their own machinery for use in Bournville. Barrow was responsible for another innovation. When he began his job he noticed that there 'seemed to be no drawing of the Works and its machinery, except the fire insurance plans'. He resolved to make a drawing of each room with its working parts, but 'needless to say it never got done: for there were many other things claiming attention'. Not surprisingly, Barrow later appointed ' a real draughtsman in the person of Arthur Hackett'.

('Fifty years Ago. Some Reminiscences of the Engineering Department', BWM, June 1937, pages 189-190).

In 1905 a major step was taken by the establishment of a Cost Office. Led by A. E. Cater, its people priced each of the factory's operations. They assessed direct costs like labour, machinery and materials and the amount that should be paid towards the overall running of the works. In this manner the cost of each line was made plain, ensuring 'the scientific regulation of the price of goods'. The establishment of the Cost Office had other results. It led to 'an organisation for producing factory records, a requisitioning system, a central receiving deck, stores,

official stock and "running out" lists, stock control and the appointment of checkweighers.' By 1914 other departments included Wages, Labour, Buildings, Manufacturing, Inspection, Sales, Export, Statistical, Planning and Chemists.
('Mr Edward Cadbury', BWM, January 1944, p. 1)

The emergence of departments was matched by the recognition of a proper management structure and by the setting up of committees. The first were Men and Women's Suggestions Committees, started in 1902 after George Cadbury Junior had been impressed by similar American schemes for taking up good ideas from the workforce. As employers, the Cadburys were noted for their attention to their employees. As early as 1893 a canvass had been taken of the women workers to see whether they preferred to abandon 6.00 a.m. starts and instead begin and leave work at later times. The switch was supported overwhelmingly and it was brought in. Still the new committees did represent an important move. They were permanent and were embodied within the company's official framework. Within a short time they included three representatives elected by the workers, another important new principle.

These initiatives were followed three years later by the formation of a Men's Committee, chaired by George Cadbury Junior. It had ten members, eight of whom were staff and foremen appointed by the directors and two of whom were elected by the foremen themselves. Similarly a Women's Committee had seven members chosen by the directors, one representing the Men's Committee, and two elected by the forewomen. It was chaired by Edward Cadbury, a man who had a deep interest in women's work in general. In 1905 he wrote an article on this subject for the General Federation of Trade Unions, and the next year he co-authored a major study: *Women's Work and Wages. A Phase of Life in an Industrial City.* Amongst his other achievements were the formation of a Girls' Social League (1909) which strove to improve working conditions for young women in Birmingham; and investigations into sweated industries, which helped to lead to the government creating Trades Boards to regulate wages in such occupations.

Both committees met weekly and the directors delegated 'many matters' to them. According to Edward Cadbury, 'that was the beginning of the devolution of responsibility from the Board to Committees, including such matters as the inspection of the Works, holiday arrangements, etc.' Amongst the other committees formed later were those relating to Sales and Buying. Like the Suggestions Committees, they also came to have elected representatives and were seen as steps towards 'more democratic control' of the company. The First World War slowed down this trend, but in 1917 two Drafting Committees were organised, each with an equal number of managers and workers. Their task was to bring in a feasible scheme for the creation of Works' Councils, one each for the male and female workers.

These came into effect in October 1918, based on the principles of democratic voting and the equality of employees and management. The fundamental effects on working relationships was stressed by a Miss Muscott at the annual meeting of the Women's Council in 1952.

Girls' Works Committee, 1907.

Chemists' department, 1905.

It must almost be impossible for you to realise what a revolution such changes meant . . . the formation of committees representative of Workers and Management who would deal with the Works rules and regulations, welfare and recreation, suggestions and sickness benefits, to mention only a few functions. ('From a Woman's Point of View', BWM, April 1952, p. 1).

The Works Councils were supported by Shop Committees, one for each department, on which the foreman or forewoman was a member. Their objective was to bring 'workers and management into as direct contact as possible' and to achieve 'the human touch'. In this way workshop problems could be considered 'from the point of view of the individual and not the mass'. In 1965 the Works Councils merged, and four years later the new body was unionised. It disappeared in the late 1970s, although the principle of consultation and co-operation has continued to be supported actively.

Such far-reaching actions were supported by education schemes designed 'to train the workers so that they will be able to take more responsibility'. From the summer of 1906 all educational work was centralised and co-ordinated, whilst the Bournville Works Education Committees were created. Within four years it was a condition of employment for all young workers to attend evening classes until the age of eighteen. These became voluntary in 1913 after the establishment of mandatory Day Continuation Schools for boys at Stirchley Institute. Later moved on to the Friends' Hall in Cotteridge, the headteacher was C.J.V. Bews. From 1919 girls were taught under Miss Cater at the Beeches. Six years later all day classes were brought to a modern college on the Green at Bournville. Compulsory attendance at these was not ended until 1971. There was a variety of other learning measures like Training for Forewomen and Office Training, whilst the Education Committee arranged scholarships, lectures and weekend schools.

(Edward Cadbury, 'A Quarter of a Century's Survey', BWM, March 1924, p. 74).

Adhering to the religious beliefs of their founder John Cadbury, the company initiated schemes to encourage thriftiness amongst its workers. These began in 1897 when it was decided to celebrate Queen Victoria's diamond jubilee by opening a savings account for each employee. All those who had been with the firm for three or more years received a gift of 20s, and those whose length of service was less were given 10s. This scheme ran until the First World War when a branch of the Birmingham Municipal Bank was opened at the factory. Another important move came in 1909 with the introduction of holidays with pay for men and boys who had been in employment for one year or more. The entitlement began at three days pay, increasing to seven days for those with five years service. An extra day was added for each additional five years of work. It was 'welcome news'.

With ten days liberty in prospect and nothing coming in the family man must needs 'think twice' before arranging to take wife and children away for a change; in point of fact it means either draining a deep draught from his savings or foregoing the said change; the new scheme

The firm arranged facilities for employees to purchase Savings Certificates, by buying the certificates and allowing the employees to pay for them in instalments. The minimum instalment was 2d per week per 15/- certificate. The employees had the added advantage of receiving interest on the certificate from the date they were purchased by the Firm.

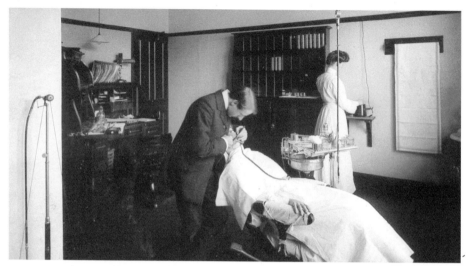

Dr. J. Jenkins Robb, M.D., was appointed in 1905. Here is the surgery of those days, which occupied one of the cottages built for employees in 1880, and was close to no.2 lodge. (1905)

"May Day" decorations (1st May 1906), showing the horse vans for Birmingham deliveries, the original "Sentinel" steam van, and the first petrol van, a "Dennis". (1906)

fortunately brings the luxury of a seaside holiday in closer prospect for many, and no one, we imagine, will be more glad than the Firm themselves to see the large number of sun-tanned faces returning to work after the general holidays. (BWM, July 1909, p. 240).

The scheme did not rely on contributions from the workers themselves. It was a gift from the company. Unsurprisingly, the employees held a mass meeting to acknowledge this generosity. Within a few years holiday pay was extended to women and girls. By 1911 they were also included in the pensions schemes which had been initiated for the male employees five years previously. In the same year a woman doctor was appointed to complement the Works Doctor who had been employed since 1902. Bournville also boasted a dental department, whilst the company operated a Convalescent Home for Women in Bromyard, Worcestershire. A similar place for the men was opened in 1922 at Harlech.

Organisational innovation was matched by continued developments in the buildings of Bournville. By 1910 and despite increased mechanisation the employees of Cadbury Brothers had increased to 5,300. It was obvious they needed more space. A new stock room, despatch deck and warehouse had already been constructed and in 1911 they were joined by the multi-storey 'M' Block and by the one-floor 'Q' Block. On the north-Eastern side of Bournville, 'Q' Block was divided into three sections for the printing of labels, card-cutting and the making of boxes.

Down the centre passes a raised gangway, and the view from this, as one looks down on the heaps of brightly coloured paper, the piles of finished, or partly finished boxes, and the girls sitting or moving about in their white caps and overalls, is one of the most vividly picturesque sights in Bournville. Even more impressive is . . . the amazing and intricate machinery which is now used in card-box making. In particular, it is impossible not to be fascinated by one machine which takes in a plain piece of strawboard at one end, and turns out a completed box at the other. (Williams, The Firm of Cadbury, p. 80)

'Q' Block was later extended and in 1914 it was joined by the multi-storey 'T' Block. Methods of transportation did not change as drastically. Horses remained essential, although in 1901 Cadbury did introduce a Thorneycroft Steam Van. Four years later it also boasted a petrol-driven Dennis motor vehicle.

The continued expansion of Bournville was assured by the company's drive for new products. In 1906 Bournville Cocoa came onto the market in response to a demand for a cocoa flavoured with spices and treated with alkalis which intensified its taste. Two years later a dark Bournville Chocolate block was brought out, but there was little doubt which new line was the most important. It was Cadbury's Dairy Milk. Launched in 1905 it was not the firm's original milk line. Eight years previously a milk chocolate had been produced by mixing granulated sugar and milk powder with cocoa mass and butter. Taken from a melangeur, the mix was ground to a paste and forced into moulds, each of which was levelled off with a knife. The result was an eating chocolate which was coarse and dry. It compared badly to a rival product made by the Swiss chocolate maker Daniel

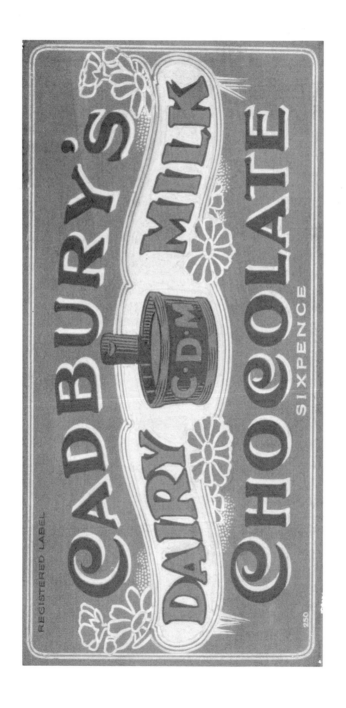

An early Cadbury's Dairy Milk wrapper.

Peter who used condensed milk. Alert to the high sales of the foreign brand in the United Kingdom, in 1901 Cadbury Brothers informed their travellers that 'we are still giving much time and attention to experimenting and are determined if possible to bring out something better than Peter's'.

In a move reminiscent of his father's trip to Holland in the 1860s, George Cadbury Junior went to Switzerland to learn about 'more up-to-date processes and plant for condensing milk'. When he returned, Cadbury installed a large milk condensing plant at Bournville and soon brought out a new milk chocolate bar. It failed to dent the supremacy of its Swiss rival. A team of experts strove to develop a chocolate 'with a far higher milk content than any previously known' and to lay plans for its production. Led by George Cadbury Junior, it included N. P. Booth, the chief chemist; Otto Unger, confectioner; Louis Barrow, engineer; and Harry Palmer, foreman.

The new line was ready by June 1904. A trio of names were considered for the new product, with 'Dairy Maid' winning out over 'Jersey' and 'Highland Milk'. However, before the bar was launched the name was changed, as explained by Mrs E. M. Creacy. Her parents were owners of a confectionery business in Plymouth.

One day I was admiring and enjoying a packet of Swiss milk chocolate, then a novelty, when Mr George Sara, a well-known commercial traveller called for Cadbury's. I showed him my chocolate and he tried a piece and said: -

'This is very nice - but wait a couple of journeys; we are bringing out a new chocolate that will sweep the country - Cadbury's Dairy Maid.'

'Dairy Maid', I replied, 'I wonder you don't call it Dairy Milk - it's a much daintier name.'

He immediately wrote the name in his order book. About six weeks later I was delighted to receive a large slab of Dairy Milk Chocolate addressed to me personally from Mr Sara, and I knew my idea was approved.

('Who Suggested The Name?', BWM, July 1955, pages 212-3).

Whatever the origins of the name Cadbury's Dairy Milk, also known as C.D.M, did take the market by storm. According to Laurence Cadbury, 'the darker milk chocolate was pushed into obscurity' and by 1917 it had almost disappeared. In the process the Swiss monopoly was broken.

(L. J. Cadbury, 'The "C.D.M" Story', BWM, August 1955, p. 244).

The creaminess of the new chocolate was emphasised by the wrapping on the bar. Printed in gold and black on a pale lavender background, the words 'Cadbury's Dairy Milk Chocolate' encircled a tub of milk on the front of which were the letters 'C.D.M'. Half-penny bars were packed for retailers in boxes with a distinctive and intriguing design on the label. This had a pixie skimming the cream from a bowl of milk. Such eye-catching advertising was accompanied by a series of outstanding posters created by a local artist, Cecil Aldin. The early ones focused on the qualities of Cadbury's Cocoa, emphasising it was 'the most refreshing and nutritious of all cocoas'. The effective and attractive promotion of the company was accompanied by the registration of a distinguishing trademark - a tree with the word 'Cadbury' stretching across to its trunk. There was a belief that this was based either on the cocoa tree or on a line of trees on hill close to Cadbury Camp in the West Country. In fact it was made about 1905 by the French artist Georges Auriol, who also designed monograms for authors and musicians such as Ravel and Debussy. The tree was used on presentation boxes, tableware and other promotional items such as milk jugs until soon after the end of the Second World War.

(E. H. Keen, 'Letter', BWM, January 1944, p. 19).

'Dairy Milk' was as vital to the growth and success of Cadbury as had been 'Cocoa Essence'. George Cadbury Junior himself had ensured that new machinery would be ready for its production. He suggested to the board that it authorise an output of twenty tons a week. His fellow directors thought this was too ambitious and asked for just five tons. Yet George Cadbury's confidence was justified. By 1914 sales of C.D.M had multiplied tenfold and it had become the firm's major line, whilst the use of dairy milk chocolate had boosted greatly the output of Easter eggs. Two years later a milk assortments brand was launched. The chocolates were put onto trays in special 5¹/₂lb boxes and sold loose to the customers at 3¹/₂d a lb. In this way the line became known as 'Milk Tray'. A ¹/₂lb, deep-lined box was introduced in 1916. Known as 'the box for your pocket' it was followed by a 1lb box eight years later, so creating a market for popular boxed chocolates.

The original, softer flavour of Cadbury's Dairy Milk gave the firm a major boost in the chocolate market and led it into further expansion. Crucially in 1911 operations were begun outside Bournville when a milk condensing factory was opened at Knighton in Staffordshire. No longer would milk be brought directly to Birmingham, instead it would be handled 'on the spot'. This was for three reasons. First, the production of dairy milk chocolate requires only the small proportion of milk which is not water. Rather than send bulky loads of milk to Bournville it was more cost effective to have a factory in a milk-producing area where the solid matter could be extracted. Second, this process lessened the possibility of milk spoiling on a long journey in hot weather. Third, the stream at Bournville was so small that it was liable to be clogged up with milk effluent, making the water unfit for use in the processing of the milk. Knighton was more effective because it had a bigger stream.

Two years later another milk factory was set up at Frampton, Gloucestershire. Both plants were alongside canals, to allow economical transportation to Bournville. By the mid 1930s they had been improved and enlarged and were handling 17,000,000 gallons of milk a year. Other milk factories followed at Marlbrook in Herefordshire, Bangor-on-Dee in North Wales, Llangefni in Anglesey and Rathmore in Ireland; whilst from 1921 a site at Blackpole was acquired so that the saw mills, tin stamping, nut departments and various stores could be transferred from Bournville.

Although machinery and techniques have improved since Cadbury's Dairy Milk was

A typical chocolate packing room of the 1910 - 1915 period. 'J' and 'S' Blocks had bridges across them, but otherwise this might have been any of half-a-dozen or more large boxing rooms. (1910)

Knighton Milk Factory showing the canal. The early corrugated iron buildings were extended by buildings in brick or timber. (1925)

sold first, its basic production remains the same. Today top quality cocoa beans are bought mainly from Ghana and taken to Chirk in North Wales. Here the raw material is processed to make the cocoa mass containing about 55% cocoa butter. The mass is taken to the milk factory at Marlbrook where it is mixed with full cream milk and sugar and then condensed into a rich, creamy liquid. When dried it becomes a milk chocolate crumb which is transported to Bournville where it is mixed with further cocoa butter, tempered and then moulded into the final product - Cadbury's Dairy Milk.

The use of milk as a major raw material was matched by a shift in the policy of purchasing cocoa beans. Until the dawn of the twentieth century, most supplies were bought from the Caribbean, South America and the Portuguese-owned West African islands of San Thomé and Principe. In 1902 Cadbury was offered an estate on San Thomé, 'quoting amongst the assets some hundreds of labourers at a given price'. Disturbed at the thought that these people might not be free, the company carried out investigations which revealed that the cocoa plantations on the islands did use slave labour. The Cadburys decided that their personal and business ethics did not allow them to continue with the trade. Faced with the loss of a major source of cocoa beans, attention focused on the Gold Coast as a possible source of imports. Now Ghana, its produce did not have a good reputation and 'Bournville had never even risked a sample purchase'. The reasons were simple: merchants in the capital, Accra, offered one price for cocoa irrespective of its quality; whilst payment was made by a chit which could be redeemed for goods in the merchant's store.

(W. A. Cadbury, 'Cocoa Cultivation and its Relation to Bournville Trade and Prosperity', BWM, August 1936, p. 262).

In 1909 William Cadbury himself visited the region and talked with the chief of the Eastern Provinces, the Konor Mata Kole. It was a momentous meeting.

> At that time Gold Coast cocoa was of so low a standard that Bournville hesitated to buy at all, but the visit to Odumassi gave great hope for the future, for there for the first time I handled Gold Coast cocoa of the first quality. The chief . . . was a keen agriculturist, and personally supervised his own and his people's farms. His sister showed me the cocoa butter that she herself had extracted from the beans.

(W. A. Cadbury, 'A Distinguished African', BWM, March 1939, p. 89).

A long-standing friendship was made as well as a mutually beneficial business relationship. In 1910 a Cadbury representative was sent to Accra. He was instructed to pay the market price in cash for cocoa which was carefully fermented and dried. Shipments soon began and within thirty years cocoa from the Gold Coast was essential to Cadbury's. By then 95% of the cocoa bought was Grade 'A' quality.

(W. A. Cadbury, 'Cocoa Cultivation and its Relation to Bournville Trade and Prosperity', BWM, August 1936, p. 262).

This intimate relationship with the Gold Coast led Cadbury into various community ventures such as the provision of scholarships for African students at Achimota College and the building of hostels and village halls. Such schemes reflected the deep-seated belief that the business of Cadbury had an obligation to the people with whom it was connected. In particular, George Cadbury and his wife, Dame Elizabeth were crucial in setting up a number of organisations which are still serving Birmingham and the wider world. They bought a large house in Northfield, turned it into an open-air hospital and gave it to the Birmingham Cripple's Union. Known as the Woodlands, it is now the Royal Orthopaedic Hospital. In 1910 they paid for the construction of Bournville Infants and Junior Schools; and the next year they opened the baths in Bournville Lane, the land for which had been given by the company. They also gave over one of their homes, Woodbroke, for the study of social and religious work in an international atmosphere, so laying the foundation for the internationally-renowned Selly Oak Colleges; and in 1909, George Cadbury was influential in establishing Fircroft College for working men.

One of the most celebrated of his achievements was as a housing reformer. His wife evoked his passion for good homes in an attractive environment.

> When I first came to Birmingham we lived at Woodbroke and I would walk with my husband through the fields and farmland between our home and the works planning how a village could be developed, where the roads should run and the types of cottages and buildings. ('Memories of Old Bournville', Cadbury News, July 1986, p. 2)

George Cadbury resolved to avoid the developments which were transforming the nearby villages into suburbs of Birmingham. In Stirchley, Cotteridge and elsewhere builders were constructing treeless roads filled with long terraces in which each house had six rooms - one above the other, tunnelling back from the footpath. They were a great improvement on the badly-built and unhealthy back-to-backs of old Birmingham but they were too monotonous and dull for George Cadbury.

Determined to make his dream a reality, in 1895 he bought 120 acres on which he erected 143 houses to be sold at cost price with the help of low interest loans. These were followed by the building of houses to rent. Then in 1900 he established the Bournville Village Trust. He was:

> desirous of alleviating the evils which arise from the insanitary and insufficient accommodation supplied to large numbers of the working classes, and of securing to the workers in factories some of the advantages of outdoor life, with opportunities for the natural and healthful occupation of cultivating the soil.

The Trust had control of 330 acres and set about erecting carefully-thought out houses in a rectangular cottage design. The aim was to establish a mixed community and not one based only on employees. Well-built, spacious and sanitary, they were open to air and light and were grouped in pairs, threes or fours and set back twenty feet from tree-lined roads. There were gardens to the front, vegetable gardens to the back and one-tenth of the estate was reserved for open spaces. This careful town planning had astounding effects. In 1915 Bournville's infant mortality rate was 47 per 1,000 live births. This compared with an awful figure of 187 in the poor, central Birmingham

The first Bournville Cottages, erected about 1880.

A view of Linden Road. 1902

district of St Mary's. Similarly the general mortality rate was an outstandingly low 8 per 1,000 people, contrasting with 24.5 in St Mary's.

(Carl Chinn, Homes for People. 100 Years of Council Housing in Birmingham, Birmingham 1991, p. 23).

George Cadbury was not the only industrialist to consider the provision of good-quality houses, but he was probably one of the first to appreciate the significance of the setting of dwellings. W. A. Harvey was the architect for the trust and he made it plain that Bournville ought 'to stand as an example of what the village of the future might hold. A village of healthy homes and pleasant surroundings where fresh air is abundant and beauty present.' Bournville did become an example and was visited by Ebenezer Howard and others associated with the Garden City Movement. During the inter-war years, the Bournville Village Trust continued its activities by developing parts of Weoley Castle and Northfield. It still plays a major role in social housing by adhering to the principles of George Cadbury whilst ensuring that it relates to the needs of a changing society.

('Bert's Work is Now Complete', Cadbury News, September 1987, p. 2).

In their involvement with grand projects, neither George nor Elizabeth Cadbury neglected the importance of helping individuals like Mrs M. Bartley. She was:

one of those poor children (Birmingham-born of a family of seventeen) who used to travel in a coal boat up the canal to the party at Cadbury's farm. And what thrills and excitement we used to receive! This party used to be known by us children as 'up the Cut in the coal boat to Cadbury's Farm.' I look back on those wonderful days of my childhood with great pleasure. ('Up the 'Cut' to Cadbury's Farm', BWM, July 1955, p. 1).

Such parties had taken place since the 1880s, when George Cadbury had set up a large tent for the entertainment of poor children in the gardens of his home at Woodbrooke. After his move to the Manor House in Northfield, the parties were held in the grounds and in a specially constructed 'Barn' which held up to 700 people. This concern with the well-being of children was shown clearly during the First World War. Dame Elizabeth Cadbury was chairman of a committee which cared for twenty-five Serbian boys who had escaped from the Austrian armies. Some of them were sent to Bournville Village School, others to a school in Kings Norton. After the war they returned home and Dame Elizabeth was awarded the Serbian Red Cross of Honour.

Obviously the First World War had a profound effect on the business of Cadbury Brothers Limited. Within two days of the outbreak of hostilities the commandeering of horses made it difficult to deal with parcels, and within six months there were worries about a shortage both of raw materials and labour. These problems worsened as the war dragged on. One result was an increased reliance on female workers. Eveline Pitt was forewoman in the fruit room when she agreed to marry Harry Ward early in 1917. Formerly of the electrical department at Bournville he was now in the Royal Navy. As her daughter explained, there was one sad note affecting Eveline's plans for the wedding: her marriage meant that she would have to leave her job.

As a last resort, and being of indomitable spirit, she requested an interview with Mr George Cadbury

Bournville Children's Festival : Fancy Dress Parade and procession through the Village. (1909)

Some window showcards of the early 1900's

and explained to him that when her new husband went back to sea after his leave she would be living exactly as present, in her parents' home but would have to work at another place, after having given up the job she loved and comrades she had worked with. After listening to what she had to say, Mr Cadbury said, 'Why don't you wait until the war is over Eveline?', to which she replied, 'Can you tell me, sir, when that will be?' He shook his head. Eva continued, 'We have no idea when the war will end but Harry asked me to marry him on this leave. There is always danger at sea and he may not even see the peace. That is why I don't want to wait.' My mother told me that Mr Cadbury was so long in thought that she grew quite apprehensive, then he said, 'Eveline, you must submit your notice and leave in accordance with the rule. When your sailor returns to his ship come back and your job will be waiting.' (Peggy Woodroffe, 'Letter to Ken Taylor', 27 July 1997).

Eveline Ward remained at work until her husband was demobilised.

Many employees were members of the Bournville Works Ambulance Corps, which had been established with the encouragement of the firm's doctors. In 1917 this body became a division of the St John's Ambulance Brigade. Its members performed invaluable tasks by acting as orderlies at hospitals and by transferring wounded soldiers from trains to ambulances. W. H. Taylor was one such injured man. Arriving at Bournville Station 'one beastly wet night in April, 1918' he was placed into a motor vehicle by the St John's Ambulance Brigade. He was 'astonished and pleased' at seeing a large crowd of girls and women from Bournville who 'gave us a hearty cheer', as they did each time transfers took place.

(BWM, January 1932, p. 7).

More than 2,000 Bournville men joined the armed forces and the firm insisted on keeping in close contact with them. Each combatant was sent periodical parcels of books, and 'as far as possible, the type of literature was selected to suit the recipient'; whilst they were delivered with woollen hats, scarves and socks knitted by women employees. Twice a year the men received 1lb of chocolate, usually Mexican, and crucially the company augmented the government's allowances to the dependants of its fighters: married men's allowances were made up to two-thirds of pre-war average wages and single men's to one third. At the end of the war, the discharged and demobilised Cadbury workers sent an address to the directors, desiring 'to render the heartfelt thanks of all for the practical sympathy and kind solicitude shown us in so many ways during our absence, also for the financial support granted in the form of allowances to our dependants, which relieved us of our greatest anxiety, and for the gifts and comforts sent out to us in all parts of the world'. The vast majority of men went back to their old jobs, whilst 36 who had become disabled were sent on educational courses or manual training 'to fit them for special occupations'. Where necessary, convalescent home treatment was arranged. Within a year of the peace, these men and all the other workers of Cadbury Brothers Limited were involved in a momentous business merger.

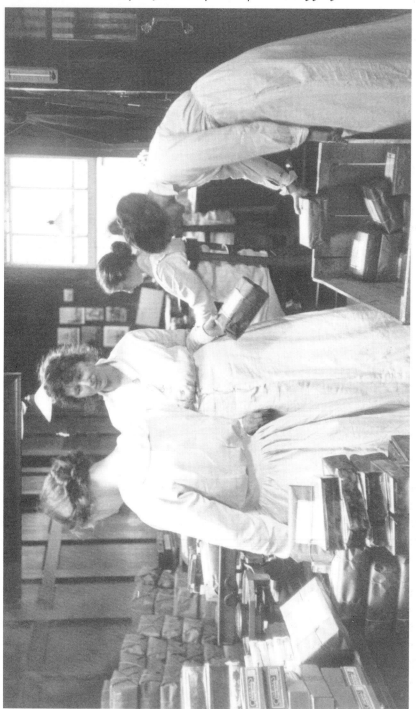

The Firm supplied chocolate and books to employees in the Forces, and the Education department was responsible for this work.

Chapter 4: An International Business, 1919-1939

The coming of peace in 1918 signified the emergence of Cadbury as the United Kingdom's chief producer of chocolate and cocoa. This position had been wrested from Fry of Bristol, which had been the market leader for over a century. The enterprise dated back at least to 1756 when Joseph Fry, another member of the Society of Friends, had advertised his services both as an apothecary and as a maker and seller of chocolate. Eight years later he bought the well-established and successful chocolate-manufacturing concern of Walter Churchman. By 1777 Fry was based at premises in Union Street and after his death, his son Joseph Storrs, gained the business a reputation for innovation and quality.

Under his descendants the firm expanded rapidly, opening other factories in Bristol and bringing out new lines such as chocolate cream bars in 1866. Thirty years later it became a limited company with a registered capital of £1 million and 4,500 employees - almost twice as many as Cadbury. Yet Fry was faced with a major problem as was made plain by Sir Egbert Cadbury. In 1919 he left the Royal Air Force and with no vacancy at Bournville he applied to his family's main competitor for a position. Arriving for the first time in Bristol, he thought he knew what the chief works in Union Street looked like from the composite picture used in Fry's advertisements:

in these it was shown situated alongside the harbour and connected with the railway. I found, however, that in actual fact at Union Street there was no railway and no dockside, and that the factory was an ordinary-looking building in an ordinary street in the centre of the city.

In total, Fry's had twenty-four premises scattered around Bristol. Not one had a right angle and all were built 'on curves and of odd shapes, following the lines of the streets'. This inefficiency of the buildings was compounded by outdated plant. The two works which made chocolate and cocoa were powered by a steam engine in the basement, 'driving a vertical shaft - a magnificent example of millwrighting, but it had the great disadvantage that when it was necessary to stop one machine, the whole factory stopped!'

Hindered by a variety of old, inadequate works which were hemmed in by narrow streets giving inferior transport links, Fry's sites compared unfavourably with Bournville. Cadbury's locational advantage was accompanied by a growing reputation for pioneering products and machinery - a standing which had been held once by Fry. By the turn of the twentieth century the Bristol firm had lost its clear dominance of the industry and 'about 1916, after a hard and bitter chase', it was overtaken by Cadbury. The crucial factor in this reversal of roles was the determination of the Birmingham business to concentrate on the quality of their products during the hard trading conditions of the war - 'at a time when many firms were more interested in output'. Within two years of Cadbury gaining the lead, J.S. Fry decided to merge its financial interests with those of Bournville and the British Cocoa and Chocolate Company was formed to hold the ordinary shares of the two concerns. The superior organisation of Cadbury was indicated clearly in 1919 when A. E. Cater was transferred to Bristol to set up a Cost Office and take over sales from one of the Frys. In the next year the decision was made to move production to a purpose-built factory in the countryside. Sir Egbert Cadbury and Louis Barrow were entrusted with the task of finding a suitable place. Taking a map they 'walked along the railway line in the direction which we thought most likely to produce a site'. They came across it at Keynsham, mid-way between Bristol and Bath. It was an excellent choice: close to large centres of population from which it could draw its workers, it was served by first-class rail and road connections and was bounded on three sides by the River Avon. Untrammelled by later restrictions on building in green-field areas, excavations began in 1921. Two years later, following 'an embarrassingly successful' public competition, the new factory was called Somerdale.

In 1934 the last of the Bristol factories was closed down and the shift to Somerdale was completed. Despite the move and the introduction of successful new lines such as 'Crunchie' (1929), Fry struggled throughout the fiercely competitive inter-war years. It went into liquidation in 1935 and became a wholly-owned subsidiary of Cadbury run by a Somerdale Committee, including Sir Egbert Cadbury and five directors from Bournville. During the Second World War all the plant and machinery at the West Country factory were dismantled and taken away for the war effort. When they were returned they were put down afresh without the firm having to meet 'the tremendous cost of a job of that magnitude'. Sales increased considerably in the post-war period so that by 1956 customers were buying 203 tons of Fry's products for every 100 tons sold in 1938.

(Sir Egbert Cadbury, 'The Firm of Fry', BWM, June 1957, pages 204-5).

Cadbury's eclipse of Fry was matched by the growing international status of the Birmingham enterprise during a difficult period for commerce. The First World War had brought exports almost to halt, so leading many nations to encourage the expansion of home producers. After the peace the powerful marketing position of such firms was strengthened by the widespread imposition of tariffs which hobbled competition. Cadbury was affected badly by this restriction of free trade, especially in a number of Commonwealth countries. The company reacted imaginatively to these adverse conditions. First, it united its interests with those of Fry in Canada, South Africa and the Irish Free State. In Australia, a third partner was James Pascall Ltd - the well-known sweet manufacturer of Mitcham; whilst in New Zealand it was R. Hudson and Co. of Dunedin.

Second, Cadbury established works abroad. The first of these was on the Claremont Peninsula of Tasmania, near to the island's capital of Hobart. Opened in

Left to right: P S Cadbury, W Barrow, W A Cadbury, E Cadbury,
G Cadbury, B Cadbury, Miss D A Cadbury, G Cadbury, Jun, L J Cadbury,
M Tatham (secretary). (1921)

The man on the second desk away from and facing the camera is George Dean
Oyston who many years later became head of the Export Office. (1907)

1920 the factory was remote from the main Australian centres of population in Sydney and Melbourne, but it was not affected by the high temperatures of the mainland and so artificial cooling systems were not needed. Technicians, foremen and forewomen were sent out by all three companies involved in the venture, increasing the already high costs of beginning production. Just as the initiative began to pay its way it was hit severely by the Wall Street Crash and the world depression which followed in its wake. Sales of Claremont's products fell by half, but picked up with the emergence of the Australian economy from the slump. Before the outbreak of the Second World War a new block had been erected at the works and it was giving employment to 1,000 people.

By this date Bournville lines were also in production at factories in Montreal, Canada; Port Elizabeth, South Africa; Dunedin, New Zealand - where Cadbury had amalgamated with R. Hudson and Co. in 1930; and Ossory Road, Dublin. The Irish works was opened in response to a sudden and unexpected raising of import duties from 5¹/₂d to 2s per 1lb on 2 May 1932. According Dr A. W. Sanderson of the Cadbury Export Department:

> This meant that the firm would have to pay the Irish Government 6d a 1lb more than they received from the Irish trader - not a very sound business proposition. In case this should not be a sufficient deterrent, they imposed in addition the famous Package Tax of 2d per package imported. One wrapped Neapolitan was ruled to be a package within the meaning of the Act.

Fortunately the Irish authorities were supportive when Cadbury decided to manufacture their goods locally. Whilst the new factory was constructed, the firm was allowed to import cocoa at the old rate of duty, so long as it was tinned in the Irish Free State. When it was completed in 1933, the new works was used for roasting, grinding and making cocoa, Drinking Chocolate and Bourn-vita. Six years later another factory was brought into operation at the East Wall, close to the Dublin docks, for the grinding, conching and moulding of goods.

(Mr M. Tatham, 'Bournville's Overseas Factories' and Dr A. W. Sanderson, 'Establishing an Overseas Factory', BWM, August 1939, pages 250-9).

The building of factories abroad was matched by the development of the Cadbury system of depots around Britain and Ireland. Those at London, Manchester and Glasgow were opened first, followed by that at Liverpool on 26 May 1925. Situated in the North Mersey Goods Station of the London, Midland and Scottish Railway it consisted of two floors. On the ground floor was a loading deck of about 228 square yards which had rail and road access; and on the first floor were two sections. One contained the main stockroom, offices and the assembly area for orders, whilst the other had a reserve stockroom and message room. From these buildings supplies were sent out to a district stretching from Southport in the north to Runcorn in the south.

('The Firm's New Depots', BWM, April 1926, p. 104).

Dublin depot. (1926)

Some of the hand-covering of Grade I lines was done on these "stones" - granite table-tops, highly polished, and heated by steam. These girls are decorating the units they have covered. The stones were used for a number of years, but went out of use soon after this view was taken, being replaced by individual bowls and steel tables and racks. (1922)

A delivery of Cadbury's chocolate to the shop of Mary Louise Francis in Barn Street, Birmingham. (Thanks to Margaret Adler).

The site emphasised the alertness of Cadbury to the importance of good transport links in the growth of its business. W. A. Lewis was a junior clerk at Bournville when George Cadbury Junior and Mr A. G. Marsden inaugurated the depot scheme. Before then goods were 'despatched mainly in cases'; afterwards they were sent out in bulk via stock containers carried by trains. There were several advantages to depot system. Goods arrived in the shops more quickly and were fresher; there was less risk of damage or theft in transit; and the labour and material costs of separate packing were eliminated.

('Evoking Memories of Early Days', Cadbury News, February 1989, p. 2; and Major Egbert Cadbury, 'Some Aspects of the Transport Problem', BWM, February 1946, p. 32).

Within a year the Liverpool depot had become so successful that its warehousemen were increased from four to ten. Three years later it had been joined by depots in Dublin, Leeds, Newcastle-on-Tyne, Cardiff and Belfast, and by 1939 there were sixteen of them within the United Kingdom. Able to give prompt service to customers frequently ordering small quantities, the depots quickly gained new trade and became essential to the progress of Cadbury. In 1922 rail had transported a massive 83% of the goods supplied nationally by Bournville. This compared to just 4% delivered through the depots. Eight years later there had been a dramatic switch in these proportions, with the depots and their vans sending out 75% of the total products. Unsurprisingly an increased dependence on motorised transport led to the rapid decline in the use of Cadbury's horse-drawn vehicles. They disappeared in the early 1930s with the retirement of the last carter, Henry E. Bishop.

('George Cadbury, 'Depot Developments', BWM, July 1930, p. 214.)

Cadbury's expansion nationally was emphasised by its purchase of R. S. McColl Ltd, with its 167 shops in Scotland and its factory in Glasgow. Still the continuing success of the business was mainly reliant on its principal manufacturing centre - Bournville. As in the period before the First World, the factory was associated with new lines which captured changing trends in the public's taste for chocolate. The first of these was introduced in 1920 and was called 'Cadbury's Dairy Milk Flake'. Formed out of folds of chocolate which made it crumbly and flaky, it came to be associated with the name '99'. According to Basil Murray, a former archivist at Bournville, this arose because in its early days 'Flake' was an 'un-named miscellaneous line whose recipe was registered in ledger number 99'.

There are other, more colourful explanations. John Nedwell, of the firm's display section, recalled that in the 1930s a Cadbury salesman gave a sample of a 'Flake' to an Italian shopkeeper. So impressed was he with the chocolate's taste and texture that he declared it was a '99'. In Italy this accolade was given to anything considered the best because the Pope's elite Vatican Guard had 99 soldiers. Another account gives John Chadwick the credit for the name. In the 1920s he was a Cadbury salesman who covered the Dundee area and he is supposed to have suggested to an

Italian ice-cream seller that 'Flake' could be placed on top of plain ice cream as an alternative to peaches, pears and other fruit. He called his innovation '99' after the shout for 'top of the house' in bingo.

('How Did 99 Flake earn Its Unusual Name?', Bournville Reporter, October 1980, p. 2; 'Bingo Name For Flake', Bournville Reporter, December 1980, p. 2; and 'Flake Name Came from King's Guard . . . or Bingo', Bournville Reporter, January 1981, p. 2).

Soon after the introduction of 'Flake', Cadbury began to make Easter eggs filled with fondant or marshmallow and in 1923 whipped fondant eggs were brought out. Costing $3^1/_2$d each, they were within the reach of most people - as were milk chocolate marzipan eggs costing 3d and 6d and marketed from 1938. These products were mass-produced using methods adopted about 1900. The machinery included a rotary machine with an automatic measure, hinged moulds, a spinning device for coating the mould evenly with liquid chocolate and a rapid chilling process. Larger Easter eggs were also made. Those which were hollow were moulded in one piece, whilst those which were filled were made in two halves. Using sugar and marzipan, these eggs were decorated intricately with animals and flowers. Obviously they were more expensive, but the most splendid and costly of the Easter eggs was the 'Cadbury Continental'. Manufactured with the finest eating chocolate and filled with dark, continental chocolates, it weighed 2lbs and 'was beautifully foiled, beribboned and packaged in a presentation casket'. Each of them was sold for the large sum of 10s.

('Two Thousand Years of Easter eggs', BWM, March 1955, p. 75).

Innovations were obvious in other lines. In 1928 'Cadbury's Fruit and Nut' moulded chocolate bar was launched, followed five years later by 'Cadbury's Whole Nut'. Then in 1935, as it did with all national celebrations, the company acted decisively to recognise the silver jubilee of King George V. Since his accession Cadbury had sold a 'King George' assortment box and in the year of the festivities it launched the 'Queen Mary' and 'Empire' boxes. They were accompanied by the 'Jubilee Selection', based on the selection boxes sold annually at Christmas. There were two sizes containing several of Cadbury's most popular moulded and confectionery goods as well as a portrait of the King and notes about his reign. The firm also brought out tins containing either Bournville or milk chocolate. They were aimed at schools and other public bodies which wished to present children with a souvenir of the jubilee, and 'special printing could be added to link the gift with the donor'.

('The Firm's Jubilee Lines', BWM, May 1935, pages 160-1).

The designs on chocolate boxes in general continued to reflect the high artistic standards associated with Cadbury since the 1860s. In 1933 the company commissioned 'a number of artists of distinction' to put forward ideas for the covers of boxes. Amongst the successful designs were 'Pixie' by Arthur Rackham, a world-famous illustrator of children's books; 'Ring' by Dame Laura Knight, the most

Bournville girls cheering T. M. King George V and Queen Mary when they visited Bournville in May 1919.

C.D.M Blocks emerging from the cooler to be wrapped. (1930)

celebrated female artist in England; and 'Still Life' by Mark Gertler, an outstanding painter of the modern school. The work of these and other artists did not diminish the importance of Cadbury's own Design Office headed by Miss B. E. Lindsay. She had joined the firm in 1906 and was responsible for the look of the 'King George', 'Prince of Wales' and 'Princess Elizabeth' boxes as well as many Christmas boxes.

Miss Lindsay retired in 1934. Within four years, her successors in the Design Office were responsible for the appearance of an eye-catching blue pack decorated with a red rose. It contained a quarter of a pound of fifteen different chocolates, each of which was wrapped in foil and brightly-coloured cellulose film twisted at both ends. Called 'Roses', the pack was available either in plain or milk chocolate and it was designed to appeal as a 'thank you gift'. Selling at 2^1/$_2$d for a quarter, the new brand swiftly became one of the most important of Bournville's confectionery goods. Its success was due to a number of factors associated with the prosperity of Cadbury in general. 'Roses' was a well-researched, quality product which was packaged attractively, sold competitively and marketed effectively.

At the annual Traveller's Conference in 1930 the significance of advertising was stressed by Paul Cadbury, the son of Barrow - then Chairman. He had been appointed to the Board of Directors a decade before and since then he had been responsible for sales. A pioneer of modern marketing techniques, his message was unequivocal: 'It pays to advertise. It pays to sell advertised lines. It pays to show advertised lines.' Travellers played a crucial role in the implementation of all three slogans, as he made plain with a theatrical message:

A modern car dashes on to the stage. Out of it leaps a spruce young representative of today. In a stride he is at the shop window noting with quick attention its contents, both the goods and the advertising material displayed. As he enters the shop his printed order book is already being whipped out and with it newspapers opened at the latest 'ads' of the Firm, and 'pulls' for the shop window . . . The young traveller dashes out again to the car for samples to show new lines, and the curtain descends leaving him also booking an order item by item. ('Travellers' Conference', BWM, July 1930, p. 212.).

Sales techniques were backed up by national advertising campaigns. The most effective of these was initiated in 1928 when a poster appeared which both showed and told the public that there were '1^1/$_2$ Glasses of English Full Cream Milk in Every ^{1}/$_2$lb of Cadbury's Dairy Milk Chocolate'. Almost thirty years later, the editor of the Bournville Works Magazine justifiably claimed that 'the idea of expressing visually, in the simplest possible terms, a plain fact about our milk chocolate was one of the most brilliant conceptions in the history of the Firm's advertising'. Through newspapers, magazines, television and cinema, the glass and a half symbol became familiar not only in the United Kingdom but also throughout the world. Soon it needed to be accompanied by no other word than 'Cadbury's'. So effective was the image of the 'glass and a half' that it was used regularly until 1965. Twelve years later it was relaunched and it remains a feature of Cadbury's modern advertising. *('The "Glass-and-a-half" Generation', BWM, February 1957, p. 51).*

A coupon scheme was another aspect of Cadbury publicity. It had been introduced in 1906 as part of the sales drive for the new product of Bournville Cocoa. By the outbreak of the First World War it had been extended to Cocoa Essence and Breakfast Chocolate. Customers gained a coupon with each purchase and when they had collected a sufficient number they were rewarded with a box of chocolates, a cocoa jug, a whisk or a caddy. Cadbury reluctantly adopted this initiative, forced into doing so by the actions of their competitors. It was an expensive way of advertising but it did bring in extra sales. During the war the scheme was abandoned, resuming in 1924 - once again under pressure from rivals. Applying only to Bournville Cocoa and Cocoa Essence, customers soon could choose as their reward either well-known packings of chocolates or household and personal items.

Unlike the coupon scheme, Cadbury eagerly went into film advertising. Encouraged by the explosion both in the number of picture houses and cinema-goers, the firm made its first production in 1910 called 'A Day at Bournville'. Within two years it was joined by a colour film, 'The Food of the Gods', which was taken in the West Indies and looked at the cultivation of cocoa. After the war the first film was of the visit to Bournville of King George V and Queen Mary on 21 May 1919. It was a momentous occasion which recognised the significance of the Cadbury brothers not only to industry but also to social work. In front of a huge gathering of workers and onlookers gathered on the Men's Recreation Ground, George Cadbury was presented to the royal couple by the Lord Mayor of Birmingham. The King decorated several employees with the orders and distinctions they had gained during the war, and then he and his wife were guided by George Cadbury on a tour of the works and the village. Later films included 'A Tour of Bournville' (1926), the first advertising sound film; and 'The Bournville Story' (1951), made to show the public the firm's greatest advertising asset - the works itself.

(Mr C. H. Whittaker, 'Some Features of Our Advertising', BWM, July 1931, pages 105-6).

Such vigorous promotion of the company's goods was accompanied by a rise in sales even during the worst years of the Depression. In 1930, a year after Wall Street had crashed and plunged the world into economic crisis, Cadbury achieved a record tonnage of home sales. It did the same again in 1931 and continued to do so each succeeding year. Such remarkable progress was achieved not only because of strong sales campaigns and the introduction of new lines, but also because of a marked reduction in the prices of Cadbury goods. In 1928 an unwrapped C.D.M Bar, weighing about 1^{1}/2ozs, was sold for 2d. Eight years later the same sum bought a 2oz C.D.M Block, 'that is a block 50% heavier and wrapped - much more hygienic and convenient'. Similarly in 1920 a half-pound block of 'C.D.M' had cost 2s; whilst by 1933 its price had dropped to 8d. This competitiveness was enabled by a massive fall in the cost of raw materials such as cocoa and sugar; by a drop in transportation costs; and by increased efficiency in production achieved by mechanisation. *(Mr F.J. Berry, 'The Changing Aspects of the Factory', BWM, August 1936, p. 243).*

Amongst the most important additions to the plant were the automatic moulding machines which doubled the output of each employee from 1927. Once made, the blocks were also wrapped automatically on machines operated by women like Molly Manton. She told how:

. . . they are wrapped first in metal foil, then in an airtight wrapping gummed at the edge, then in a purple and gold wrapper. The machine on which I work wraps 80 of these blocks every minute . . . People often ask me 'do you find it monotonous doing the same job all the time?' Well, no, because although you might think that every day appears to be the same, the same noise of the machines, the same miles and miles of chocolate bars and blocks from the Moulding Department, I've got so used to it that I can talk and joke with my friends as I work. That makes every day different and I enjoy it. (Food Factory. The Story of One of the World's Largest Food Factories , Told by Some of its Workers, Birmingham about 1938, pages 16-17).

In spite of the significance of machinery, many jobs still could be carried out only by hand. These included the skillful stacking of bags of cocoa beans into towers higher and wider than a three-storey house; the careful grading, sieving and blending of beans; and the artistic decoration of chocolate cremes.

Workers who actually made Cadbury goods were supported by a wide-range of other employees. Night watchmen patrolled the factory and kept an eye out for fire and burglars; workers in the Trades Departments ensured constant production; 'mobile men' kept wrapping machines supplied with material and trolleyed away finished goods; post boys delivered over 5,000 messages a day; stockroom people found the goods for specific deliveries; despatch men sent out the orders; and clerks like Miss Ruby Price processed invoices. She began at Bournville in 1927. Her first job was on the shop floor 'hand-wrapping the little make-weight chocolates that went into assortments'. After a month she was transferred to the General Office, later to be known as sales accounts, where a plain writer was used to print addresses on accounts. After ten years service she gained a green tie for her overall which marked her promotion to clerk in charge of a section. Later she was awarded blue collars and cuffs, indicating that she was deputy chief clerk. In 1947 she was the first woman to become chief clerk and in 1966 she was appointed as head of 'one of the company's most important functions, making sure the bills go out and the cash comes in'. Five years later she retired. During her time working on accounts she had seen punch card machines replaced by Holleriths (1948) and then these give way to computers. *('From Office Girl to Head Girl', Bournville Reporter, August 1971, p. 3).*

Cadbury's production and its marketing strategies were enhanced by an acute awareness of the concerns and demands of its customers. Thus when the weight of blocks and bars was increased it was soon realised that they became too hard to break. Within a year the company had countered this problem by bringing out a milk bar with sixteen divisions and costing the low sum of 2d. Such a rapid reaction reflected Cadbury's keen attention to the majority of its consumers. In 1934 Paul Cadbury explained that:

> At Bournville we cater for the man in the street, his wife and family - the poor man at the gate rather than the rich man in his castle. For though we are very pleased to sell the landlord a box of 'Carnival', our prosperity depends far more on selling the farmer who rents the land a box of 'Milk Tray', the ploughman who tills it a '2d Bar', and his wife a tin of cocoa. (Paul S. Cadbury, 'The Consumers of Chocolate', BWM, p. 77).

Children were also recognised as essential to Cadbury's prosperity. During the 1920s the company published the first of the Elsie and the Bunny books, in which a young girl is magically taken to Bournville to see how cocoa is made and to eat chocolate. This action was followed in 1934 by the introduction of specially- designed tins of cocoa. A free miniature animal was given away with each tin purchased and youngsters excitedly collected 'Nutty Squirrel', 'Dan Crow', 'Monty Monkey' and others. The success of the scheme encouraged Cadbury to start its Cococub Club in 1936. Within two years it had 300,000 members, each of whom received a monthly magazine. The organisation of sand-drawing competitions in the summer was another imaginative idea of the late 1930s. In fifty seaside resorts around Britain, children drew a wide-range of pictures associated with the company - from a glass and a half to characters from the Cococubs. Impartial onlookers acted as judges and the winners were given Cadbury chocolate vouchers.

Despite the expanding sales of its chocolates, Cadbury did not ignore the importance of drinks to the company's success. A new beverage called Bourn-vita proved popular from 1932. Made with malt extracted from barley, full-cream milk, the finest cocoa and eggs, it was pushed as a 'food drink'. Although Cocoa Essence was slowly disappearing from the market, sales of Bournville Cocoa were so buoyant that a modern Cocoa Block had to be built in 1928. Five stories high and with 187,000 square feet of floor space, it was the largest cocoa factory in the world. Norman Bennett, a millwright, began work there when its floors were bare. He believed that the block:

> was perfectly designed for cocoa-making. For by feeding raw materials in at the ground floor and elevating to the top floor then through machines to the lower floors the law of gravity will bring the finished product out at the bottom. At its peak we were producing 250 tons of Bournville Cocoa, and as many as one and a quarter million cans rattled through the tin tracks in a week. ('Norman's 42 Years in Cocoa Block', Bournville Reporter, September 1970, p. 1).

Norman helped to install thousands of tons of machinery needed for the roasting, cleaning and sieving of cocoa beans. It was used until his retirement in 1970.

The Cocoa Block was part of a massive construction programme which led to the rebuilding of three quarters of Bournville between 1919 and 1939. Inevitably most

Sand drawing competition contestant. (1938)

of the original factory disappeared. During 1936 alone, the old Cocoa Essence Department, Plain Chocolate Room, Cost Office and other sections made way for the erection of 'U' Block. This adjoined another new facility, 'V' Block, opened in 1934. Other inter-war buildings included the Power Plant (1921); 'L' Block (1922), 'O' Block (1925); Dining Room Block (1927); Moulding Block (1928); and Chocolate Block (1934). Care was taken in the design of these structures. In particular, all the manufacturing rooms had rounded corners between walls and floors so that cleaning was easier.

Waxing demand ensured that Cadbury continued to require extra workers. By 1938 the company employed 10,000 men and women at Bournville alone - 2,500 more than in 1919. Each morning they were called to work by a "bull" which sounded at 7.35 a.m. They had ten minutes to enter the factory through one of four lodges. This daily scene was vividly described by Tom Insull.

The hooter, however, was a signal for the dykes to be opened and a torrent of tradesmen - a posse of painters, plumbers and printers, battalions of biscuit makers and bricklayers, millions of moulders and marzipan experts, crowds of clerks, creme beaters and cracknell creators were all poured forth . . . (Tom Insull, 'Main Street', BWM, April 1928, p. 120).

Throughout the factory high and constant quality was demanded and expected. Researchers strove continually to improve methods of obtaining the smoothest chocolate possible. Annually they carried out 150,000 tests whereby particles of chocolate were magnified under a microscope and examined for absolute regularity and satisfactory fineness. Chocolates which were not approved had to be reground. Rigorous checks for purity and suitability applied to all raw materials. Each year chemists made 8,000 tests on milk to make certain that it was rich enough in cream; 20,000 samples were taken of other ingredients and manufactured products; and every consignment of sugar was assessed for moisture and purity.

Similar stringent tests were made on the foodstuffs used for the centres of chocolates, as a Cadbury scientist stressed in a description of a typical day of his work.

Soon I hear that a member of a large business house in London may call to see me. He has some samples of Orange Oil. This is obtained from the ripe oranges in Italy and is used, together with orange marmalade, to flavour orange cremes and marzipans. These new samples of oil seem to be very good, but before we buy any I must examine the samples carefully in the laboratory. All my tests must show that they are of the best quality, but before it is used in the factory I shall myself make some orange cremes with it to taste the flavour. Now a storekeeper brings me a tin of pineapple. It is just like the pineapple you have at home. before he can give any of it to the confectionery foreman to make pineapple cremes and cubes I must make sure that it is not stringy or tough and has the real delightful flavour everyone enjoys. (Food Factory, p. 23).

The same scrutiny was applied to apricot, strawberry and blackcurrant jams, West Indian limes, Chinese ginger, almonds, honey, walnuts and other products.

An Inspection Department ensured that quality was maintained as the raw materials were turned into Cadbury goods. Sixteen inspectors were employed. They were 'competent with eye, nose, and palate, and have the power to stop the use of anything - whether ingredients or manufactured products - which is not of the standard quality'. Before they left the factory, the finished chocolates, confectionery and cocoa were tasted by members of a Quality Committee. All of them had 'delicate palates and sound judgements' and for two hours each week they used them. Each taster only ate a quarter or an eighth of a chocolate and each had the power to tell the confectioners to change an ingredient.

(A. W. Knapp MSc., F.I.C., 'Quality and the Factory', BWM, August 1935, pages, 267-9).

Workers on the shop floor played a vital role in safeguarding Cadbury's exacting standards. Foremen and forewomen scrutinised production and were expected to call attention to any changes they noticed. Women in the manufacturing rooms were not allowed to powder themselves, use nail varnish and perfume, or wear beads, flowers, flags, tokens, pins and rings with stones. Before they left work at night they had to completely cover all trays of chocolate and confectionery with a clean dust sheet. Realising the importance of hard-working, conscientious and careful employees, the company was thoughtful about whom it took on. Marjorie Malley started at Bournville in March 1931:

And Cadbury's only took school leavers. At the end of every term, you know, the local schools used to sit for written and medical tests and if you passed you were very lucky as the wages then were 11s 10d a week where most of the other firms paid at the most 10s a week. And if you weren't accepted on leaving school you'd got no chance whatsoever as only school leavers were accepted and you had to attend Bournville Continuation School for one full day every week until the age of 18 . . . Discipline was very strict, but they did look after your welfare, you know, resident doctor and dentists. And we had good sports and social activities provided. And if you went in to the Dining Room before 7.30 a.m. as work started at 7.40 you were given a free cup of cocoa and two slices of bread and butter in case people had come without breakfast . . . Once you were in at Cadbury's you were never sacked unless you did something drastically wrong.
(Carl Chinn Show, BBC Radio WM, 27 July 1997)

Because of its safe working conditions, good wages and secure employment Bournville appealed to many working-class Brummies. They were also attracted by the commitment of both the firm and the family to its workers and the City of Birmingham. This sense of duty was highlighted in 1931 when Cadbury celebrated the centenary of its founding. On the afternoon of Friday 19 June directors, workers, pensioners and relatives of people concerned with Bournville all gathered on the Men's Recreation Grounds to hear a speech by the company chairman, Barrow Cadbury. He explained that:

A special display in a seaside hotel, to which all local customers could be invited.
(1927)

Barrow Cadbury at the Centenary. (1931)

This Centenary has already been celebrated by the gift of a large open site to our City for the purpose of hospital extension and public playgrounds - by the issue of two centenary histories of the Firm, the erection of historical cartoons in the restaurant, and the work carried out on the Village Green, and I have been asked by the Directors to announce that, in order further to mark this great day in the Firm's history, they have decided to distribute £50,000 . . . The gift will take the form of National Savings Certificates. These can be cashed, if desired, but if, as we hope, they are held, they automatically appreciate in value year by year. ('The Centenary', BWM, October 1931, p. 160).

One other factor enhanced the popularity of Bournville as a place of work. This was the involvement of members of the Cadbury family in the life of the factory. According to Marjorie Malley, the men 'had to do so much time in every department, dirty jobs as well as clean'. She remembered that Dorothy Cadbury, a director from 1919 - 52, was 'a lovely woman who . . . worked in an office the same hours as all the employees'. The magnetism of Bournville was stressed by Ted Smallbone who grew up nearby in Cotteridge. Throughout the locality, 'it was every mother's dream that her boy or girl would get a job at Cadbury's'. He did so in 1924 aged fourteen, and as he put it 'Cadbury's was an ideal employer as employers go'.
(Howard Wilkinson, Toolmaking and Politics. The Life of Ted Smallbone - an Oral History, Birmingham 1987, pages 11-19).

Five years after entering the firm, Ted went to Austria with the Works Youth Club. Like the others on the trip he saved for his own fare and board, but 'Cadbury's also paid for you for being away from work because they granted you that holiday'. Dick Leadbetter, later the company's representative in Leeds, was also a member of the Bournville Youths Club. In 1920 he took part in its first seaside camp at a village between Barmouth and Harlech. Most of the lads had never been on a train or seen the sea. The weather 'was appalling, gale force winds blew down most of the tents, and rain thoroughly soaked the camp site. But none of us minded, we carried out the full programme of climbs and excursions and had the time of our lives'. Another popular activity was the 'School on a Barge' initiated in 1917. Derek Ager participated in the event in the mid 1930s, just after he had began work in the card-cutting department. He recalled that he and other lads spent a week on a narrow boat 'fitted out as a schoolroom and which conveyed us to different towns where we visited factories and local industries'.
('A Walk Down Memory Lane', Bournville Reporter, August 1979, p. 6; 'Working at Cadbury is a Real Education', Cadbury News, November 1994, p. 2).

Within Bournville workers were able to take advantage of improved facilities such as larger recreations grounds at Rowheath, a new concert room, a library and reading rooms and a lido, also at Rowheath, which was opened by Edward Cadbury on 3 July 1937. Mrs Harper was one of the many girls who made full use of the opportunities provided by the company. An active member of the Bournville Girls' Athletics and

Camp at Polzeath, near Wadebridge, Cornwall. (1947)

The Addressograph Office was a small adjunct to the General Office in 1925.

Social Club, for just 2s membership she had 'free use of equipment, plimsolls and tennis racquets' and was able to join numerous classes. She had no doubt that through her job she enjoyed a social life she would never have experienced otherwise.

('Letters', Bournville Reporter, November 1979, p. 6)

Soon after Mrs Harper began work at Bournville, George Cadbury died. She remembered him as a 'dear, very endearing' man who walked through her department each morning. Always 'cheerful, bright and alert', he wore a fresh flower in his button hole and said 'Good Morning' to everyone he met. The whole workforce mourned his passing. In a fitting tribute, W.E. Cossons described George Cadbury as a man 'whose monuments are all around us'. He was 'a great creative genius' whose talents had been vital in the phenomenal growth of Bournville. Yet for all his commercial success, George Cadbury was always concerned with the welfare of others. For that reason he would be 'remembered not only for what he himself did but for what he inspired and encouraged others to do'.

(W.E. Cossons, 'George Cadbury 1839-1922', BWM, September 1939, p. 1).

George Cadbury's family held fast to his principles and continued to commit themselves to doing good and serving the community. His wife, Dame Elizabeth, succeeded him as chairman of the Bournville Village Trust and carried on his work with the Selly Oak Colleges; whilst their son, George Junior, was active in the movement to provide community associations and community halls on council estates. Amongst other gifts, he and his brothers, Edward and Henry, donated an estate to the National Trust and passed over large areas of the Lickey Hills to the City of Birmingham for the enjoyment of its citizens.

The descendants of Richard Cadbury were as noticeable in public life. His elder son, Barrow, gave three of his former homes to good causes: Uffculme went to the Adult School Union; Cropwood became an Open Air School; and Southfield was taken over by the Y.W.C.A. William, his younger brother, was Lord Mayor of Birmingham from 1919-21. During this time he organised one fund to help the unemployed in Britain and another to give relief to distressed people in Europe. After his term of office ended he carried on as a hard-working and concerned councillor. In 1938, the year in which Birmingham celebrated the centenary of receiving its charter of incorporation, William received the municipality's greatest honour. He was made a freeman of the city - an appropriate appreciation of his family's past and continuing service to Birmingham. This honour was conferred a year before both the city and Bournville was transformed by the Second World War.

This last portrait of George Cadbury, who died in 1922 was taken by Whitlock.

Chapter 5: Bournville at War, 1939-45

With the declaration of war on 3 September of 1939 a host of works throughout Birmingham were turned over to military production. The Austin sent out aeroplanes, machine gun magazines, service helmets and much else; Dunlop made military tyres; amongst other things, Lucas manufactured rotating gun turrets and sten gun magazines; whilst the B.S.A. was responsible for so many rifles that when the factory was badly-bombed it gave grave concern to the Prime Minister, Winston Churchill. The significance of these firms was matched by that of other big companies such as the Morris Commercial, Fisher and Ludlow's, the Wolseley and Kynoch's. A variety of smaller businesses also made vital contributions. The hooks and eyes company of Newey Brothers turned out clothing fasteners for the armed forces; Samuel Heath and Sons shifted from making brass bedsteads to producing blow lamps, firing pins and paraffin stoves; and J. Hudson and Co. supplied whistles to the Royal Navy, the Army, the Royal Air Force, the Merchant Navy and the Civil Defence.

Yet the war effort was not restricted to metal-working concerns and even Cadbury became deeply involved in the struggle for freedom. Many of its employees were transferred to jobs of national importance at other factories; the Blackpole works was taken over by the government, whilst the Battersea Depot in London was given over to war work; and parts of Bournville itself were handed over to Lucas, Austin and other firms essential to military production. Then in the late spring of 1940, the directors of Cadbury acted to ensure that the company itself played its part in the survival of the nation. The outlook for the United Kingdom was grim. France had fallen, the United States of America was neutral, the Soviet Union had a Non-Aggression pact with Germany and the prospect of an invasion by the enemy loomed. At this low point, Bournville Utilities Ltd was formed to use sections of the factory and its material resources to carry out work for the Supply Departments of the British Government.

Two thousand workers were transferred to the new company. They were involved in a wide-range of occupations. During the war engineers made fifty-three vertical milling machines for rifle factories, specialist machinery for Lucas, the main parts for 200 horizontal milling machines and over a thousand jigs and tools for various firms and Ministries. These skilled men were also involved in making parts for guns and aeroplanes, a task later taken over by women transferred from the chocolate and confectionery departments. The Moulding Department itself switched to the manufacture of cases for aeroplane flares, ribs and gun-door assembly for Spitfires and air-intake and super-charger controls for Stirlings. Sub-assembly work for other aircraft was carried out by the Light Metals Department, whilst its sheet metal counterpart concentrated on producing pilots' seats for Defiant fighters, junction

An ex-chocolate maker turning Hydraulic Jack Ram Spindles for "Tempests."

Testing Anti-Aircraft Rockets after filling.

boxes for Wellington bombers and upper-mid-gun turrets for Stirlings.

By late 1941, Nissen huts had been set up on the canal bank close to Bournville. In these 350 women and seventy-five men filled anti-aircraft rockets with explosives. When the contract for this job ended the employees shifted to the covering of aircraft petrol tanks with layers of rubber and rubberised material which rendered perforations self sealing. This work was taken on from Dunlop when that company was ordered to concentrate solely on making tyres for the military. Twenty-five types of fuel or oil tanks were covered - from sixteen gallon versions for Beaufighters to massive 1,150 gallon tanks for Vosper motor torpedo boats. Still, Bournville's biggest job of the war was the assembly of 5,117,039 service respirators and 6,335,454 canisters. Six hundred workers were involved, of whom only fifteen were men. Margaret Smith was one of the female majority. As a sixteen-year old her job on gas masks required 'speed and accuracy and was especially suitable for nimble-fingered girls'. Margaret was also an auxiliary nurse. Once a week she and other volunteers entertained 'war-wounded men in a huge corner of the canteen'.

(Margaret Smith, Some Memories of a Northfield Woman, unpublished manuscript, no date, p.10)

Bournville was camouflaged from the Luftwaffe with wire netting which was easily lifted off after the war. Employees were trained as roof spotters to look out for enemy planes, others learned to be fire watchers and yet more joined the Special Constabulary, and decontamination, light repair and rescue squads. A unit of the Home Guard was also established. Norman Sabin was seventeen when he joined it

As soon as the air raid siren went we rushed to the top of block six to the look out post, ready with five rounds of ammunition - to shoot the enemy down. But nothing ever happened, we never fired a shot in anger. We used to keep watch up there at night too and phone down to the pavilion headquarters telling them where bombs were dropping. (Frances Vines, 'Factory's Own Dad's Army', Bournville Reporter, July 1979, p. 7)

Fortunately no attacks hit the buildings, although one night in December 1940 a bomb did damage the bridge carrying the canal over Bournville Lane. Reporting for work the next morning, Daisy M. White and her friends were asked to go to 'D' Block 'to sweep away the flood water from the canal'. The water was cold and smelled horribly, and as they brushed it away there were 'dead cats and rats floating about'. *('Memories . . .', Cadbury News, September 1994, p. 2).*

Cadbury and its workers were active in other aspects of the war effort. As part of the 'Dig for Victory' campaign, the football pitches at Rowheath were ploughed up for the growing of wheat and vegetables; other fields were given over to the grazing of sheep; and the Bournville Village Trust made land available for allotments. During air raids elsewhere in Birmingham, members of the firm's St John's Ambulance Unit played an important role. Harold Willmot was one of them. He was on duty at the Odeon in town 'one terrible night when the police called us to Worcester Street which had been flattened'. The injuries were appalling and Harold learned more 'about first

A Light Repair and Rescue Squad

Women at Work
As the War went on more men's jobs
were taken over by women, some
working on night shifts.

Recruits for the Home Guard unit based at Bournville.

aid and dealing with severely injured people that night than in the rest of my life'. He and his comrades found people in shelters crying out for help. They worked until all their supplies were used up and then 'had to walk home next morning as all the roads were blocked by fire engines, hoses and debris from bombed buildings'.

(Harold Wilmott, 'The Brigade Faces the Blitz', Cadbury News, October 1992, p. 2).

During such attacks, Cadbury sent out 'mercy vans', vehicles filled with urns of hot cocoa. Miss Cook, the Chief Demonstrator, was in charge of these cocoa caravans, one of which was manned by Robert Broom and his colleagues. Members of the firm's Home Guard, on one occasion they arrived in the centre of a raid: 'down a street shelter we went issuing out cups of steaming cocoa'. Inside the conditions were terrible, 'condensation was running down the concrete walls, and the smell was not very pleasant'. Although bombs were dropping, he and his mates 'could not wait to collect the cups and get outside into the fresh air, albeit less safe'.

('Memories . . .', Cadbury News, September 1994, p. 2).

Along with its war work, Cadbury continued to produce chocolates and to take on youngsters. Ken Taylor was one of them. Aged fourteen in 1944 he picked up:

> *15s a week, that included 10s basic wage and 5s piece work and you had to work hard for that five bob. When you became 21 years old you were given a man's wage, some of the older blokes picked up as much as £3 10s 0d a week. On pay day, which was always Friday, all us workers congregated around the departmental office at about a quarter to twelve, waiting for the foreman to come with a sealed metal tray with all our wages in. On top of each tin was stamped a check number and when the gaffer called out your number, you went and got your tin and emptied out your money. If it was alright you put your tin back, if it was wrong you held on to your tin until you could tell the gaffer your wages were wrong. (Ken Taylor, Cadbury Collection Storyboard, 'Cadbury World').*

The war not only influenced wages. It also forced the company to change its policies towards female workers. Barriers were broken down between the men's and women's departments and married women were given full-time posts. Their employment rose after 1945, so that by 1952 there were 600 of them at Bournville compared to 2,300 single women. Over the succeeding years married women became more noticeable. By 1962 they constituted two-thirds of female employees - although 80% of them were part-timers.

(Dorothy Cadbury, 'From a Woman's Point of View', BWM, April 1952, p. 102).

Of course, the war had a drastic impact on the production of chocolates, cocoa drinks and confectionery. Sugar and cocoa beans were difficult to import - whilst as an essential food, all milk was directed by the government to the liquid market. The chocolate industry was allowed to use only small amounts of surplus milk. This was a serious problem. In 1939 Cadbury's had handled nearly 27,000,000 gallons of milk and each week had produced over 1,000 tons of milk chocolate. The company reacted to the problems it faced by cancelling all assortment and seasonal lines; by using milk

The Cadbury Cocoa Van in Birmingham, Christmas Eve 1940. Notice the bombed buildings in the background.

Some of the range of Cadbury products from the war years.

powder to produce 'Blended' and 'Ration' chocolate; and by reducing the number of standard packs from 237 to 29 by 1942. In that year the government recognised the importance of chocolate as a food and made it subject to rationing. Each person was restricted to 3oz a week, just under half of the pre-war consumption.

Measures such as these led to a marked drop in output by all chocolate and confectionery businesses, yet proportionately Cadbury was the worst affected. The firm's biggest competitors benefited both from large government orders which supplemented their civilian trade and from a transfer of tonnage from the Birmingham company. Consequently many rivals gained in output. At the same time, war-time conditions forced them to simplify their products and reduce the number of their lines. In this way they had been 'taught some of the advantages of mass production methods' and would 'become keener competitors of ours in the post-war world'. For all the problems it faced, Cadbury was determined to maintain its reputation for value for money, quality and fair dealing not only during the war but also in the peace that followed.

(Mr D. W. Collier, 'Factory Efficiency', BWM , February 1946, p. 34).

Chapter 6: Derationing and Diversification, 1945-69

Trading conditions remained difficult for several years after 1945. There was a shortage of labour; rationing remained in force; paper supplies were low; and the government continued to impose restrictions on the use of raw materials, the output of goods and the buying of new plant. These negative factors combined to make overheads too high at Bournville and at Cadbury's other works. Affairs did improve from September 1946 when the civilian sweet ration was increased to 4ozs per person, with an extra ounce available at Christmas. In the following year, although it stayed well below the pre-war figure, total production at Cadbury went up by 18%. Yet late in 1947 'this satisfactory record was clouded' by an awareness that reduced sugar supplies would mean that the sweet ration would be cut back once again to 3ozs per person.

Matters were made worse by the spread of a cocoa-tree disease which caused a fall in the availability of raw cocoa. In May 1948 it was estimated that from a world need of 600,000 tons there would be a 100,000 ton shortfall. In these adverse circumstances manufacturers were forced to pay £237 for each ton of cocoa. Such a sum was unprecedented and was at least six times the pre-war amount. The result was a reversal of the trend for lower prices for chocolates and confectionery: a block of Cadbury chocolate which had cost 2d before 1939 was now double the price - and would soon rise to 5^1/$_2$d. Cadbury directors felt strongly that such a marked increase could have been lessened if the company had been allowed to buy its own raw cocoa. Despite less of the foodstuff, they felt they had the skills and experience to make competitive purchases. They were not allowed to do so because buying was controlled by the Ministry of Food whose bureaucrats kept secret the prices it paid.

(Laurence Cadbury, 'A Year of Increased Production', BWM, May 1948, p. 1).

Battling against its problems, Cadbury brought out a new line called 'Fudge', the sales of which were boosted a year later by a welcome move by the government. On Sunday 24 April 1949 sweets were 'derationed'. The event had been long-awaited and preparations for it had been made well in advance. There were concerns that some customers would react greedily and quickly buy up the available stocks. In response Paul Cadbury made an appeal for restraint which was distributed to retailers in the form of a window card:

For seven years Chocolate has been rationed. Everyone has had a fair share but now we can buy without coupons. This is great news. Manufacturers will make as much as possible but the supply of materials is still limited. Unfortunately there is little milk for Milk Chocolate. I know that shopkeepers will treat their customers fairly, but everyone must help. Children must have the first choice, and the rest of us must use restraint in our buying. (BWM, May 1949, p. 115).

The withdrawal of the sweet ration was short-lived. Within eight weeks it was reimposed, although the amount per person was increased gradually to 6^1/$_2$ozs by July 1951. Four months later the slow recovery of the chocolate and confectionery industry was hit badly by severe cuts in raw materials such as nuts, oils, fats, sweeteners and preserved fruits. In total their availability dropped by about eighty tons each week. Cadbury was fortunate in holding large stocks of these products. Overall in 1951 it gained a 10% increase in the tonnage of goods it sold at home and abroad compared to the previous year - a result which bettered any during the inter-war period. Yet because of the obstacles faced by the trade as a whole, it was impossible to keep up this progress in 1952 - even though cocoa could now be bought on the open market.

The post-war austerity meant that Cadbury had no choice but to offer its customers less lines than before. Still there was one positive aspect to this reduction in products. The opportunity emerged for a 'review of all the Firm's labels and wrappings in relation to modern tastes and the requirements of the market'. Resolved to carry out this process carefully and professionally Cadbury consulted Norbert Dutton, an industrial designer. He had a demanding brief.

> *Modern ideas had to be linked with the traditional designs that had built up enormous public goodwill. New labels had to look well in the hand, on the counter and in the shop window. Finally, it was vital to differentiate in design between the various recipe lines, since many chocolate purchases are made not by reading the name on the label, but by immediate recognition of a familiar shape or symbol. ('Re-styling Our Labels', BWM, November 1951, p. 102).*

Dutton reconciled all these objectives. His new designs kept the traditional colours of purple and gold for milk chocolate and red and gold for plain chocolate. But instead of the previous style of capital letters, all blocks would have the name 'Cadbury's' in a standard script. Based on William Cadbury's signature, it had been used on the company's vehicles since 1921. The name of the block itself was now written in bold and without the serifs of the past.

Business prospects at home were still bleak when these new labels came into use. By contrast Fry-Cadbury's overseas position was more positive. The works in Canada, South Africa, Australia and New Zealand were enlarged and new machinery was installed, whilst a milk factory was opened at Rathmore in the Republic of Ireland. It was a bold move to prevent the 'extinction' of Cadbury's Dairy Milk. The restrictions on milk use in the United Kingdom had meant that 'since the early days of the war there has been practically no CDM in the shops and very few of the children of to-day know what real milk chocolate is - at least as we at Bournville understand the term'. Recognising that the firm's goodwill was so closely bound up with CDM, Cadbury fastened on the Republic as an alternative source of supply of milk for its best-known chocolate. Rathmore itself was in a developing milk area close to the Lakes of Killarney. It had rail access to Cork and Dublin and was close to

Coronation display of Cadbury's Chocolate. (1953)

Contributions for workers helping flood victims in East Anglia (1953)

the junction of the Blackwater River and its tributary, the Awnaskitaun. Their proximity was important as a good supply of water was needed for the processing of the milk. After its use, the water was treated and returned uncontaminated to the rivers.

('Milk from Eire', BWM, July 1948, pages 135-7).

Rathmore was joined in 1957 by Cadbury's fourth Irish factory on the Malahide Road in Coolock, Dublin. Built because extensions were impossible at the two other works in the capital, it covered about 100,000 square feet and had one long, low storey with simple lines. Light and spacious, its roof was made of pre-cast concrete. Two hundred men and women were taken on immediately to produce chocolate biscuits and four famous brands - 'Cadbury's Milk Tray', 'Fry's Cream Tablet', 'Fry's Crunchie' and 'Cadbury's Irish Rose' assortment.

('The New Dublin Factory', BWM, June 1957, pages 196-7).

By now trade had begun to improve markedly at home. In 1953 restrictions on the use of sugar were ended and sweets were de-rationed. Twelve months later milk supplies were freed up. Yet Cadbury's affairs continued to be harmed by contrary economic conditions and unhelpful government restrictions. In particular the firm was handicapped by a policy which aimed to establish fresh industries in districts of high unemployment. As Laurence Cadbury had warned in 1945, 'it is one thing to encourage new enterprise to these areas, quite another to force industries to transfer from their existing location by embargoes on their natural development'. His caution went unheeded. Like other manufacturers in Birmingham, Cadbury was not allowed to expand its buildings. This stricture stifled its ability to adopt new methods of production and to compete effectively in the export market.

(Laurence Cadbury, 'Some Current Problems', BWM, May 1945, p. 84).

By 1953, fourteen years had passed since improvements had been made in the structure of Bournville. Frustrated in its need to expand at its base the company gained a licence for erecting a factory at Moreton in the Wirral, where the government was keen to advance employment. A year later the first block was ready for the making of three million chocolate biscuits a day. Much of this was not new production but represented the transfer of most of Bournville's biscuit capacity. Fats, flour, sugar and other raw materials were delivered to the south side of the works, whilst the dough itself was processed in a baking room. Once it had been rolled into the right thickness, shaped and stamped it travelled for $8^1/_2$ minutes through 160-foot long ovens whose temperatures ranged between 50^0 and 55^0F. After cooling the biscuits were passed through enrobers, curtains of chocolate, to the packing room. By 1960 Moreton had an extra block for the moulding and manufacturing of chocolate and was giving work to 3,200 men and women. Because of growing demand for Fry's products, such as the new 'Picnic' bars brought out in 1958, another building had also been erected at Somerdale - where there were now 5,000 workers.

('The New Factory: Impressions of Moreton', BWM, October 1954, pages 317-8).

Nightmen on 'Vogue' Belt. (1955)

The BBC made a telerecording of making Easter eggs for use on a children's newsreel on the Television Service. (1955)

Chemists are seen turning over the cocoa beans and making records of temperature etc. during the experiments on a new prototype cocoa bean drier. (1957)

Cadbury instituted other initiatives to maintain profitability. In 1954 it became the first commercial business to use electronic calculators on a large scale, thus speeding up the calculation of invoices. Four years later it bought Anglesey and Caernarvonshire Dairies Limited, so gaining extra supplies of milk and a cheese factory. And although milk chocolate sales were growing and chocolate boxes such as 'Vogue', were redesigned, the company focused its assortment output on 'Milk Tray' and 'Roses' - the manufactures of which were highly mechanised and cost-effective. Such streamlining and simplification was as obvious in the making of Easter eggs. Because of a tremendous demand, the short season of sale and limited storage space, the company concentrated on 'a small number of the packings of value-for-money, all-chocolate filled eggs'. Production was improved significantly in 1955 when a continuous process was installed similar to that used for other moulded goods.

Previously a number of separate operations were involved in Easter egg production: liquid chocolate was deposited in metal moulds; the moulds were fixed to a wheel; and the wheel was turned to ensure even coating of the moulds. In contrast a new machine called a 'Mikrovaerk' allowed a sequential series of mechanical operations. Metal moulds, each in two halves, were carried on endless chains under a heater and a depositor which covered one part of each mould. A metal clamp then forced the separate halves of the moulds together. In sets of four to a frame they were taken through the cooler. The frames themselves were rotated in two directions by 'a cleverly-designed system of chains and cogs, rather in the manner of a fairground switchback'. At the end of the cooler, the frames were switched to a lower level. By the end of this return journey the chocolate halves had become hard enough to be removed from the metal moulds by demoulders. This done the moulds were sent back to the heater to begin the process once again. Meanwhile the chocolate halves of the Easter eggs were sent on a belt to the packing section where women filled them with Milk Tray assortment or Milk Drops. Finally the finished eggs were put into bright cardboard cartons.

('Two Thousand Years of Easter Eggs', BWM, March 1955, p. 76).

These cartons themselves were a recent and important innovation. In 1950 Bill Horrocks, a designer with one of Cadbury's major packaging suppliers, and John Waddington of Leeds solved the awkwardness of transporting fragile Easter eggs. They devised a carton which allowed cheap and effective movement and which did away with expensive and carefully packed baskets and boxes. Based on the open cartons used for delicate electric light bulbs, the new packaging became a prototype for development by Cadbury's own Design Office. Working on a two-yearly design cycle, its artists soon brought out cartons which highlighted the brand and which stacked easily so that they were suitable for shop display. The point of sale itself was of increasing concern to Cadbury and in 1958 it initiated the '3C Plan', Cadbury's

Counter Conversion - a major selling effort to convert whole counters in sweet shops to the effective display of chocolate and confectionery lines, especially those of Cadbury. Conceived by Charles Gillett, a salesman and great nephew of Edward Cadbury who later became deputy managing director, it was an idea that was soon adopted by all types of shop and is now almost universal. Identification of Cadbury products themselves was made more effective by changing the design of their wrappers to an upright format, to fit in with the way the goods were displayed.

('Selling Easter Eggs to the World', Bournville Reporter, March 1975 p. 5).

By that year Cadbury sales were up 70% on those for 1938. This growth was achieved by three factors: 15% came from new output at Moreton; 25% was the result of increased productivity; and night shifts accounted for another 30%. Overall, the firm's position in the United Kingdom had been helped by an expanding population and by an improving economy. Unemployment had dropped significantly, real wages were rising and people had more disposable income. These positive factors meant that each person was now buying 8ozs of chocolates and sweets compared to $4^1/_2$ozs in 1928.

(Paul Cadbury, 'The Changing Shape of Bournville', BWM, March 1958, p. 56).

A more optimistic national outlook did not lead to complacency. Increasing sales were essential to the well-being of Cadbury. Strong efforts were made to gain trade in Europe where some of the company's lines were manufactured under licence in Germany; a second factory was opened in Bombay, India to cater for growing demand for Bourn-vita and other products; and some success was achieved in the USA, with the marketing of chocolate biscuits. Still, British customers remained of prime importance and Cadbury recognised fully that the development of home demand was bound up inextricably with an effective building programme. At last in 1960, the government lifted its restrictions on construction outside its development areas so that improvements could now take place at Bournville. In particular these were essential for the manufacture of assortments, the popularity of which was burgeoning and which needed more space and labour than was necessary for the production of moulded goods.

Throughout the 1960s extensions to 'U' Block and other building work were matched by product development. Cadbury's Buttons came onto the market in 1960 itself; blocks of 'Bournville Slim', Roasted Almond and Fruit and Nut were brought out; fresh units were added to 'Roses'; and biscuit products such as 'Bar Six' were introduced. These changes were accompanied by a realisation that diversification was an essential feature of growth. In 1961 Cadbury Foods Limited was formed with Paul Cadbury at its head. The following year, after detailed market research, the company began to manufacture a variety of cakes. Determined to capitalise on its long-standing reputation for quality, Cadbury decided to use only butter for the fat in its cakes. Each carton was emblazoned with the slogan 'Baked With Butter', indicating

'U' Block West Progress. (1961)

Advertising on East African buses. (1953)

to the consumer that 'not only do we use butter but that we are particular about all the ingredients that go into Cadbury cakes'.

As with 'Cadbury's Dairy Milk', 'Flake', 'Roses' and all other of its goods, the company had ensured that the new product would be the result of 'a great deal of experimental work'. Over a period of three years, hundreds of cake recipes were tested under the supervision of Mr D. G. Broad of the Catering Department and Mr W. Schweizer, the firm's Swiss confectioner. The best of them were tasted by members of the public 'to find out which people preferred and to ensure that the most critical judgement was brought to bear on the products before setting the standards for commercial production'. Once the recipe had been chosen then engineers, chemists and production specialists had studied the problem 'of adapting processes perfected in the experimental kitchen to large-scale manufacture'. Similarly, great attention was paid to keeping the cakes fresh and to the design of their packaging. *('Now Cadbury's Cakes. Only Baked with Butter!', BWM, October 1962, pages 413-7).*

Production began in a section of the Blackpole factory and sales were tried out first in the East Midlands, backed up by·an advertising campaign. Cadbury took out full-page colour advertisments in the Nottingham Evening Post and Derby Telegraph, becoming one of the first firms to use such an approach in local newspapers. It was also a pioneer of television and wireless commercials. In 1951 the company produced a fifteen-minute programme to advertise 'Milk Tray' and 'Drinking Chocolate' on Radio Luxemburg. Called 'A Date with Dickie' it featured Richard Attenborough who went on to gain fame as a presenter. Before they became well-known, Richard Todd, Michael Pertwee and Audrey Hepburn also had experience of promoting Cadbury's goods.

By contrast, Norman Vaughan was a household name in the 1960s when he was used by the company in a long-standing campaign to market 'Roses'. He became so closely associated with the product that he was linked continually with the catch-phrase 'Roses grow on you'. 'Award yourself a CDM' also entered popular usage after a series of advertisments, whilst another favourite commercial brought fame to the words - 'All because the lady loves Milk Tray'. They were used in all action films, one of which featured the hero jumping from a sports car he was driving to grasp the skids of helicopter to which he clung as it flew across a lake. As it passed over a hotel, the hero dropped onto a hotel roof and delivered a box of 'Milk Tray' to one of the rooms.

New advertising mediums did not supplant older forms of publicity such as cinema films and spaces taken in magazines. Although they only carried a name and a reminder, posters also retained their significance. They reached 90% of all age groups in the population as opposed to 80% via the press; whilst cinema advertising, which was aimed at the 16-24/25 age group, had a reach of 70%. Through placing consistent advertisements, Cadbury maintained the best positions for its posters -

Cadbury advertising on television. The last few seconds of the advertisment generally included a "close-up" of the product.
Jane Brookfield, who won a contract after appearing in Cadbury's "Taste the Cream" commercials.

One of the famous action packed adverts for Milk Tray featuring the "Man in Black"

93

The history of cocoa in pictures

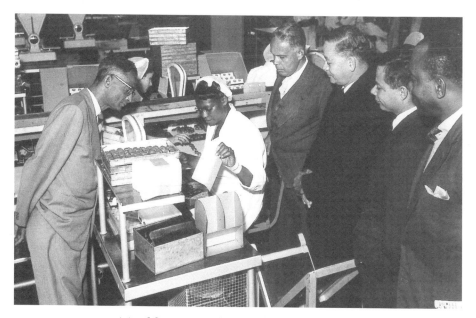

Visit of five West Indian Journalists, June 1959.

whilst their design was constantly updated. As in the past, Cadbury employed artists of distinction to work on display material, export advertising, publicity photographs, price lists, exhibitions and displays. Frank Lockwood was one of the best known of them. He started at Bournville in 1933 when there was 'an embryo advertising studio' with four artists. Their number had risen to twenty eight when Frank retired in 1958.

In the early 1950s product promotion was backed up by a permanent staff of sixty displaymen who ensured that Cadbury goods could be seen prominently in shop windows; and by 200 representatives. These men had to be alert not only to a particular advertising campaign but also to the appeal of a specific product. Thus twice as many children as adults drank cocoa, whilst overall this was seen as an unfashionable working-class drink. Consequently Cadbury pushed Drinking Chocolate as 'the latest thing', especially for young people and housewives; whilst it promoted cocoa as 'a comforting drink for cold weather and as a useful ingredient in the kitchen'. Adhering to this principle that it was best to advertise the most popular use of a product, the company 'went with the tide' in marketing Bourn-vita. As a food-drink its sales were highly-specialised and 'largely confined to women' over thirty-years old who drank it at night. Accordingly, Bourn-vita was promoted with a smiling beaker wearing a night cap. Another striking picture was used to advertise Cadbury's biscuits - that of chocolate flowing from a half-open block of Cadbury's Dairy Milk to thickly coat a biscuit.

Yet as it was pointed out by P. B. Redmayne in 1955:

Some people never read advertisments. In spite of all the trouble we take and the money we spend, we know there are people we cannot persuade to look at our press advertisments or our posters. But they come in their thousands, and with practically no persuasion, to Bournville, and this is the best advertisement we have. (Mr P. B. Redmayne, 'The Why, How and Where of Cadbury Advertising', BWM, September 1955, pages 290-3).

People had been arriving to see Bournville since 1881, but it was not until 1902 that a Visitors' Department was set up. By the outbreak of the Second World War it was dealing with 150,000 people a year, 30,000 more than the annual average in the late 1950s. Most visitors came in organised groups, often in coaches or special trains put on by British Rail between March and November. On their arrival they were greeted by Mr Major, the head of the department, and his colleague Miss O. E. Smets. Then a guide took them on a two-mile tour of the the factory and the Village, showed them a film and gave them refreshments. From 1962 visitors could also spend time in a Demonstration Room where push-button displays told the story of chocolate and Bournville. Eight years later this facility was closed mainly because of increasingly stringent health and safety regulations. These required visitors to be treated the same as employees in terms of dress and hair covering, so making trips unfeasible.

('On Show to the World', BWM, April 1959, pages 116-9).

In 1962 new delivery vans were also bought and building began on 'one of the most modern factories in the world' in Bremen. Constructed to cater for a growing market in Germany, it was to be run by a recently-formed company - Cadbury-Fry G.m.b.H.. Within three years this development had been followed by the acquisition of the Mitcham based sugar confectionery business of James Pascall Ltd, and by the introduction of 'Marvel'. An instant, non-fat milk in granule form, the new line was made at Knighton where the processing of liquid milk into crumb was phased out. Its launch coincided with the retirement of Paul Cadbury as chairman. A grandson of Richard, he was replaced by Adrian Cadbury - one of George's grandsons. The seventh head of the firm since it became a limited company, Adrian was the youngest of them to gain the position. Within four years he was leading Cadbury into a merger which was even more significant for the company's future than had been the union with Fry's.

Chapter 7: Cadbury Schweppes, 1969-90

The late 1960s was a period of company mergers, union amalgamations and increased government intervention in the United Kingdom and Europe. At Bournville there was a growing awareness that Cadbury itself needed to follow this trend to 'bigness' if it were to carry on as a strong and prosperous company. Such expansion could be attained through a number of initiatives: increased sales; the updating of existing lines; the bringing in of modern and more efficient machinery; strong and focused advertising; the raising of export sales; and the broadening of the Cadbury range by the development of innovative food products.

Progress was obvious in all these areas. The company brought out two new foods - 'Marvel' instant milk and 'Smash' instant potato. Both were innovative products carrying the Cadbury brand and soon became market leaders in their field. With Cadbury cakes, chocolate biscuits and cocoa-based drinks they formed the company's Food Division. Gains were obvious elsewhere in the business. Despite a slight fall in home demand for moulded goods and assortments, there were marked gains in selflines such as 'Buttons' and countlines like 'Fudge'. Novel 1lb and ^{1}/2lb cartons of Roses were introduced as well as Roses prepacks - bags of individual favourites including 'Nut Whirls', 'Truffle Cremes' and 'Chocolate Cremes'. The purchase of continuous machinery using a starchless moulding process made these cremes the freshest available. This was a major move forward in production. Previously starch was laid out on huge trays so that it could be impressed with hollows, into which the creme was put, once the creme was set then the starch was blown away. This process was replaced by one which used more efficient and cost effective non-stick metal moulds.

Inroads were also made into the expanding children's market by launching a well-publicised 6d CDM bar which had a free picture card inside its wrapper. New advertising was launched including television commercials for Milk Tray featuring the 'Man in Black' which were an 'outstanding success' and poster adverts for the 'Award Yourself the CDM' campaign. Finally there was an obvious improvement in exports to the USA and the Far East. Sales even rose in Northern Europe - despite the closure of the Bremen factory in 1967. This disappointment was offset in the same year by expansion in Australia where Cadbury acquired the firm of MacRobertson and its new plant at Ringwood. Near to Melbourne, this factory became the centre of production for 'Crunchie', 'Turkish Delight' and other lines, whilst the Claremont works continued to make some bars, all boxed assortments and block chocolate.

There was one other way in which 'bigness' could be achieved: through a merger. Cadbury management was mindful of the potential advantages of such a move and in the spring of 1969 the company joined forces with Schweppes, the market leader in carbonated drinks, cordials and squashes. Schweppes like Cadbury had branched out into food and had acquired such well-known brands as Kenco coffee, Typhoo tea and Chivers and Hartley jams and marmalades. The two companies had much in common. Both were long-established and imbued with a respect for past achievements yet both were responsive to the need for innovation. Both were international concerns which were associated with strong brand names. Both had made effective use of packaging and advertising. And both were intent on supplying goods of a high and consistent standard.

"This is not the case of one company absorbing another. It is a fifty-fifty agreement between two large companies who have decided it would be in their best interests to come together in order to be more successful, to grow faster and be more profitable. Joint sales of the two companies are about £260 million - and that is the size you need to be nowadays if you are to go ahead".

('It's a Merger Not a Takeover', Bournville Reporter, February 1969, p. 1).

Crucially, Adrian Cadbury avowed that the new company would 'carry on the sort of traditions to which we have become accustomed'.

Chaired by Lord Watkinson and with Adrian Cadbury as Managing Director, Cadbury Schweppes Limited had its headquarters at Marble Arch. The Cadbury and Schweppes Food Divisions were merged, so that the combined company had three main businesses - Confectionery, Drinks and Foods - with a fast-growing International Division based on exports, Cadbury's overseas operations and Schweppes' franchises. Service functions such as finance, administration and computing were handled on behalf of the whole group, but each division had to implement a firm programme of growth and development. Confectionery itself was further split into two sales forces: one responsible for marketing Cadbury brands and the other for Fry and Pascall Murray lines. Dominic Cadbury, the younger brother of Adrian, was overall Sales Director in charge of a division which annually sold 365 million bars of 'Cadbury's Dairy Milk', making it the global pacesetter; 150 million bars of 'Fry's Crunchie'; over 60 million small, fondant-filled Easter eggs; and 360 million 'Murray mints'.

For all its accomplishments, the new company could not afford to be complacent about its position. Its survival depended upon persistent growth. All divisions were urged to focus on the bettering of profits by the reduction of factory costs and the removal of unnecessary overheads. The resulting rationalisation led to the closure of the Pascall works at Mitcham. This factory had been beset by two major problems: there was no room for extra manufacturing capacity without substantial re-building; and locally there was a worsening shortage of labour. The run-down at Mitcham was spread over a long period to allow workers more time to find new jobs. Production of Murraymints, boiled sweets and pastilles was switched to Somerdale, and that of chocolate eclairs and marshmallow to Bournville.

Creme Egg sorting at Cadbury

Cocoa beans arrive at Chirk for processing

A year later, in 1971, the Birmingham factory began to take over the storage and processing of nuts from Blackpole. Workers in the Bournville unit now cleaned, graded, roasted and sorted nuts for use in moulded blocks or as the final decoration in expensive assortment boxes. Little was wasted. The only things destroyed were bad brazils and the wet outer skin from almond blanching. If something was not used for chocolates or confectionery then it was sold for cattle feed or fertiliser. The unit itself occupied four and half stories in the old cocoa block, vacated by the shifting of cocoa manufacture to a new factory at Chirk in September 1969. Situated on the Welsh border and costing £4³/4 million, it was the most modern cocoa processing plant in the world. Many of its employees were former miners who had lost their jobs with the closure of the nearby Ifton Colliery. Their tasks remain essential to Cadbury operations today.

Sacks of raw cocoa beans are unloaded onto conveyors for cleaning. The beans are then roasted in continuously-rotating gas-fired ovens. It is this roasting process which gives the beans a characteristic flavour and aroma. The roasted beans are then broken and their brittle shells discarded. The bean kernels or nibs are then hammered through a screen and ground into coarse particles. With the heat generated by the grinding process these particles become a warm paste. The paste is ground until it becomes cocoa liquor some of which is pumped into presses and the cocoa butter is extracted, leaving solid cakes of cocoa.

During the 1970s, improvements were also obvious at Bournville. Centres for assortments were now made automatically using metal moulds instead of the flour machines of the older Mogul machines; and in 1976 a new Creme Egg plant was put in which could turn out 500,000 eggs daily. In the same year new plant was fitted for the production of goods in fixed metric weights. It was used to make 'CDM', 'Bournville', 'Whole Nut', 'Brazil' and 'Fruit and Nut' in 100 and 250 gram blocks - the last of which were 1¹/2 inches longer and 10% bigger than the old half pound family size. *(Easter Eggs for Everybody', Bournville Reporter, March 1976, p. iii).*

The machinery's track carried more than 1,200 moulds on a continuous journey through depositor, shaker and cooler and then on to wrapping and packing lines. The wrappers themselves were turned out on the colour unit of an expensive Cerutti press purchased in 1968. It had a revolutionary effect. Previously the company had no option but to buy costly CDM paper ready-tinted, having to add the other colours on presses which could only print small amounts at a slow pace. Now the colour unit allowed printing from white in 'a quicker, cheaper and altogether more efficient process'.

('Making the Big One', Bournville Reporter, April 1976, p. 4; and 'Labels by the Mile', Bournville Reporter, April 1970, pages 4-5).

Packaging is crucial to all Cadbury products. A pack has to protect confectionery or chocolate from damage, deterioration from high or low humidity, foreign odours,

Now chocolate doesn't drop all over the place.

NEW Cadbury's **Curlywurly**

CARAMEL COVERED IN MILK CHOCOLATE

Because now there's a new Curly Wurly. It's just as chewy as the old one, but it's softer. So now they can bite straight through it. So now the chocolate doesn't drop all over the place. So it's better for them. And it's better for you.

New Curly Wurly from

Cadbury

T.V. Life - November 1974

insects, mould growth, temperature changes, oxidation or moisture loss. At the same time the pack must safeguard the goods from theft or loss; it needs to display them carefully and attractively so as to enhance sales; and it has to be economical.

These are not the only considerations to which the designers must attend. They are required to be aware of British and EU legislation about how a product is described, how its ingredients should be listed and the manner in which its weights ought to be referenced; and they need to be alert to the advantages of voluntary information supplied by the manufacturer. The results are impressive. Each 1lb box of 'Roses', for example has over fifty packaging elements. As it has been throughout its history, Cadbury is at the fore in meeting the challenges of a changing market whilst maintaining a steadfast grip on the qualities which traditionally have made it successful.

Subsequently, when Cadbury concentrated on its core business of making chocolate and cocoa, the company closed many of its operations on Trade Street and bought in these and other services. However, printing remained in-house longer than most others because of its significance to the Cadbury taste. Chocolate is susceptible to adverse environmental factors and it is essential that its packaging excludes taints and at the same time does not include taints. Accordingly printing must be done with low odour inks. As a result just as there are taste panels so too are there odour panels. Its members are people with sensitive noses. Their task is to smell the packaging to make sure that there is no odour.

Following the merger and the subsequent rationalisation, Cadbury Schweppes experienced two difficult years. But the company's results for 1971 were welcomed as bringing in sight the 'promised land'. Turnover was up to £296 million, a rise reflected in an increased trading profit of £23.8 million. Bournville played a major role in these encouraging figures with the making of popular lines such as 'Milk Tray', 'Roses', 'Whole Nut' and 'Fruit and Nut'. The Bournville factory also began manufacture of a popular new product called 'Curly Wurly'. Launched in 1970, it was a chocolate-covered bar designed to appeal to children both in its appearance and price. As with other original brands, before going on national sale it had been tested in a specific area - in this case the Tyne-Tees independent television region, where the adverts were fronted by Terry Scott, a well-known tv star.

At the same time in the Yorkshire TV district, 'Special Recipe' was tried out. A luxury bar made of rum, raisins, truffles and dark chocolate, its focus 'sophisticated women in the 25-45 age bracket' and it was pushed with commercials featuring titled ladies. Another 'minimum-risk product with maximum opportunity', it proved less enduring than 'Curly Wurly' which continues to be produced. There were other original lines which have not lasted. They included a popcorn called 'Hanky Panky' and 'Cadbury's Magical Dream Bar' - a white candy flavoured with ripples of banana, strawberry or orange. Changing palates and fluctuating fashions inevitably mean that not all new brands have a long life. But as in the past, the search for a fresh taste and novel look in the 1970s did lead to long-standing successes, amongst them 'Double Decker', 'Caramel' and 'Starbar'.

Throughout the 1970s overall sales were hit by the imposition of purchase tax and VAT as well as rising cocoa bean prices. Moulded bars were the worst affected by the increasing cost of this raw material - simply because they had a higher chocolate content compared to other lines. Attempting to keep the bars the same length and width, Cadbury's reduced their thickness. This strategy was criticised and consumers began to say the bars were no longer as satisfying. The company responded quickly. In 1977 the old shapes were restored and a publicity campaign was launched. Posters were put up with the familiar image of a glass and a half of milk pouring into a bar of 'CDM' but supported by the new slogan: 'You Never Tasted a Glass and a Half Like It'. Still, the main focus of advertising was a television commercial. It starred Cilla Black who held a bar of 'CDM' and sang a ditty including the words 'there's a little smile in every chunk'. All Dairy Milk wrappers carried the glass and a half symbol so as to tie in with the commercial.

The next year, 1978, Cadbury Schweppes acquired the Peter Paul group in the USA. The British company already had a factory at Hazelton, to which it now added works in Connecticut, Pennsylvania, Indiana, Illinois and California. This push for sales in North America was matched by a determined drive to increase consumer demand in other parts of the world. The export team was active in 120 countries, from the Faeroe Islands to the Far East, and in 1979 it sold 2,450 tonnes of block chocolate - up 25% on the previous year. According to Bob Crockford, then Export Sales Director, although a small amount by United Kingdom standards this was 'a great performance against a background of prices increasing by 25 per cent or more in most markets as that strong pound back home made our products more expensive in overseas markets'.

('Top Choc Bars in World-Wide Re-Launch', Bournville Reporter, 1979).

This push for fresh sales was accompanied by significant changes within the Cadbury Schweppes company in the United Kingdom. In 1980 it was decided that Cadbury itself should concentrate on the making and selling of chocolates and confectionery. All other services would be bought in. Under this initiative a variety of departments at Bournville were made redundant - printing, carpentry, joinery, engineering, card cutting and tin canister making amongst them. Elsewhere a number of smaller and older factories were shut down. Dominic Cadbury, by now managing director of confectionery, explained that the aim was to have 'fewer people, working on round-the clock, seven-day-week shifts'. The company achieved its objective.

('Modernisation Plans are Paying Off, Bournville Reporter, March 1981, p.1).

As part of the shift to specialisation, in 1986 Cadbury Schweppes sold its food,

A production line control room.

tea and coffee businesses to a management team thus allowing the main company to focus on the making of confectionery and soft drinks. In particular, the name Cadbury itself was removed from products that did not include chocolate thus allowing it to focus on its core business, chocolate confectionery. This move gave the company an opportunity to buy the up-to-date machinery and processes which were essential to the success of the new business plan.

During the late 1980s there was an investment of £24 million which transformed Somerdale; £5.5 million was also invested at Marlbrook whilst at Bournville £3.8 million was spent on a new production line for Buttons, £9.6 million on up-to-date moulding machinery, and £13.5 million on a new Creme Egg plant. Then in 1992 an expenditure of £8.7 million put 'Chirk right at the top of the latest developments in food safety and hygiene'. Bean cleaning was moved to a modern building and the main factory was provided with a new ventilation system. This prevented the entry of unfiltered air, whilst another unit ensured the high quality filtration of cocoa butter.

('Quality is Guaranteed', Cadbury News, October 1992, pages 6-7).

The results of modernisation have been spectacular. No longer is chocolate made in a series of operations, each of which was individually-controlled. Now product manufacture can be supervised from a control room filled with computer terminals and television screens. Yet modernisation has not ended. It is an on-going process. In 1993 Cadbury opened Europe's largest and most advanced chilled warehouse at Minworth, near to Birmingham. At a cost of £24 million, it is the largest single investment made in the history of the company. Built in under a year the warehouse has the capacity to store 92,500 pallets of chocolates and confectionery in a controlled humidity and at a constant temperature of 6°C.

So great is the space at Minworth that it could include four full-size football pitches, whilst if all the pallets it holds were placed side-by-side they would go from Birmingham to Nottingham. In a trade with two huge peaks of demand at Christmas and Easter, the provision of such massive storage space means that seasonal goods can be manufactured throughout the year - so maximising production and reducing costs. Significantly the construction emphasised Cadbury's deep-rooted commitment to the communities in which it is based. The Minworth warehouse uses only 'ozone friendly' refrigerants in its huge chiller units. These have less effect on the ozone layer and on the environment in general.

This continual upgrading of plant and buildings has been accompanied by acquisitions of related businesses. Although chocolate is enjoyed across the world, there are crucial differences in the types of chocolate popular in various countries. Most people prefer their national product: they have grown up with it, they are familiar with it, and it accords with their feeling of how chocolate should taste. Above all they are passionate about their kind of chocolate. For these reasons it is difficult for any chocolate manufacturer to make inroads into the export market with its own specific brands. This is why the purchase of foreign firms had been so important to the growth of Cadbury internationally. During 1988 whilst the company sold its USA confectionery assets to Hershey Foods, it made two significant foreign purchases. In Spain it took over the major firm of Chocolates Hueso; and in France, the second biggest chocolate market in Europe, it bought Chocolat Poulain. With two factories near Paris this was the country's leading maker of chocolate bars. Since then Cadbury has increased its presence in France with the purchase of La Pie qui Chante and has further strengthened its position in continental Europe with the acquisition of Piasten, a market leader in the German boxed chocolate and assortment market.

Expansion was as obvious in the United Kingdom. In 1988 Cadbury took over the Yorkshire-based Lion Confectionery, followed the next year by that of the larger sweet-making businesses of Trebor and Bassett. These additions were evidence of Cadbury's strategy to develop and extend significantly its activities in the sugar confectionery market. Bassett also brought with it Jameson's Chocolates. Its Tottenham factory turned out 'Ruffle Bars', Woolworth's 'Pick n Mix' and a limited number of gold-foiled miniature creme eggs sold without a brand. The potential of this product was swiftly realised. A quarter of a million pounds was spent on modifying their manufacture and changing their recipe. The result was the popular 'Cadbury's Mini Creme Egg'.

('Jameson's' Hatches a New Line', Cadbury News, March 199 1, p. 5).

Easter Eggs overall showed remarkable growth. During the 1980s the Easter egg market underwent a period of product innovation with Easter eggs being developed to suit every pocket, from children's eggs such as Buttons packed in brightly coloured boxes through to eggs packed with a mug and a countline such as 'Crunchie'. Cadbury's Creme Egg and Mini Eggs have both been phenomenally successful with over 300 million Creme Egg and 700 million Mini Eggs produced annually.

Product development has been as apparent at Bournville as at other works. In the late 1970s market research indicated that while consumers regarded Cadbury as the first name in chocolate their buying habits were changing. In particular there was a marked trend towards goods seen as snacks. This shift in tastes meant that at the expense of the moulded bar sector the sales of countlines were increasing. Products in this range are chocolate covered bars which are wrapped, purchased originally by the number and not by the weight. Investigations indicated that there was an opportunity to develop a countline radically different from those of Cadbury's competitors. It would be a light, textured, pure chocolate snack targeted at men and women in the sixteen to twenty-four age range.

The company's Research and Development Department was given the responsibility for bringing out the required brand. A number of prototypes were tried on consumers before the final product was achieved and a pilot plant was set up.

Known as 'Wispa' the new line was tested, as had been 'Curly Wurly', in the Tyne Tees independent television region. This area was chosen because it was a self-contained area with 5% of the total spending power in the United Kingdom. Commercials featured stars from popular tv series such as 'Hi-de-Hi', "Dad's Army' and 'It Ain't Half Hot Mum'. Salesmen were taken from other regions, a fleet of cars were hired and the area was focused on intently. The sales staff found themselves knocking at open doors. Retailers took as many 'Wispa' bars as they were able to. So great was the popularity of the new product that the pilot plant could not keep up with demand. The test was halted and the product was taken off the market whilst Cadbury executives pondered whether they ought to invest £12 million in the new plant necessary for national sales.

It was decided to take the risk. So as not to alert its competitors, a major order for new plant was not made. Instead Cadbury built its own machinery from parts bought separately, wrapping it under black covers until ready for final assembly. The result was a highly-sophisticated unit capable of making 1680 bars per minute, each of which has tiny air bubbles controlled to within 0.2 - 0.3mm. In 1983 'Wispa' went on sale nationally. The launch was backed up by a massive promotion campaign to build up brand awareness. Customers were offered mugs, pens and other popular items imprinted prominently with the name 'Wispa'. Sales were outstanding and the brand rapidly became the third best-selling countline in Britain.

Since then Cadbury has maintained its prominence as a company which develops totally new products. In 1987 it brought out 'Twirl' - a two-fingered Flake dipped in chocolate; and five years later it launched 'Time Out'. Noting the burgeoning popularity of snack foods Cadbury wanted to make a distinctive product to bridge the gap between pure chocolate snacks and simple biscuits. The key was the Cadbury taste. This meant that 'Time Out" would stand out from other wafer bars because it was covered with Cadbury chocolate with a Flake centre. A total of £12 million was invested in the bar, £7 million of which was spent on new technology and plant at Cadbury's main Dublin factory.

Somerdale has also been influential in producing original brands. In 1991 for the first time the factory made more than 50,000 tonnes of chocolates - a figure achieved despite the recession. This success was explained by the fact that a bar of chocolate still cost, on average, less than a first class stamp. Demand was especially high for 'Picnic', 'Crunchie' and 'Caramel'.

Chapter 8: Cadbury: The Master Brand

Cadbury Schweppes plc is a major international company now chaired by Sir Dominic Cadbury. Since the recent purchase of Dr Pepper/Seven Up, its Beverages stream has reached third position in the world's soft drinks market; whilst its Confectionery Stream is the fourth largest supplier of chocolate and confectionery in the globe. This strong position looks set to improve. In 1994 a factory was opened in Wroclaw and Cadbury Poland was formed. It has been followed by the construction of greenfield sites in joint ventures in Russia and China; by the starting of chocolate manufacture in Argentina; and by the take-over of Bim Bim, one of the main confectionery suppliers to Egypt, North Africa and the Middle East. Cadbury's position in Canada is even more impressive. The country was the eleventh largest confectionery market in the world in 1994 and Cadbury became its leading chocolate firm with the acquisitions of the businesses of Neilson and Allan Candy.

Within the United Kingdom Cadbury is the largest food brand linked by a single product - in this case, chocolate. The company has maintained its position by a search for new markets, such as licensing over 90 franchise products - like 'Crunchie' ice cream bars, 'Cadbury's Dairy Milk Chocolate Mousse', jigsaws and Christmas crackers. This move has not detracted from the firm's commitment to its core business and in 1996 it launched 'Wispa Gold', a bar combining 'Wispa' chocolate and caramel; 'Darkness, a plain boxed chocolate assortment and in 1997 Astros, colourful sugar coated chocolate spheres with a biscuit centre. It also brought out in 1996 the phenomenally successful 'Fuse', the biggest selling new chocolate bar since 'Wispa'. Resulting from five years of research, planning and testing, 'Fuse' contains 70% chocolate and a mix of raisins, crispies, fudge pieces and sliced peanuts. John Groen was senior project manager responsible for producing the new bar.

> *We saw this as a big opportunity to move the success of moulded recipe blocks into countlines. Then we had to decide the best way of doing it and what ingredients we should use. We went through a tremendous number of recipes - 256 in all - before we felt we had got the right ingredient combination and mix. And every one we developed had to be thoroughly tested ... We looked at different shapes of products - some early samples were cup cakes. We also considered moulded and half-moulded techniques before deciding on the sheet and cut method enrobed in chocolate.*

(*'Fuse News', Cadbury News Special, 24 September 1996, p. 2*).
In its first week on the market 40 million Fuse bars were bought.

Product innovation has continued to be important with products such as 'Wispa

*Watch the Exclusive Cadbury World Luxury Assortment being made
in our Demonstration Area at Cadbury World.*

Mint', 'Nobble' and 'Marble' whilst traditional favourites are updated and remain popular, such as 'Snack'.

The statistics of some of Cadbury's yearly sales are remarkable. If all its Easter Eggs were laid end to end they would stretch from London to Australia, whilst if every Creme Egg was stacked one on top of the other then they would reach 900 times higher than Mount Everest. Similarly more than two billion bars of Cadbury's chocolate are bought annually, and if all the 'Crunchie' bars eaten were lined up they would go from Bournville to Bangkok and back again. Each week Bournville alone produces more than 1,500 tonnes of chocolate - including 1.6 million bars of various types and fifty million 'Hazelnut Whirls', 'Almond Clusters' and other individual chocolates. There are other staggering figures. Eight hundred chocolate bars can be wrapped every minute on a single high-speed packaging machine; and in the production of 'Wispa' individual microprocessors monitor factors such as temperature at about 1,000 different points. Information is continually fed into central computers which can handle 360,000 instructions per minute.

High technology has been as crucial in the development of an innovative sales approach. In 1992 the company secured a long-term contract to supply hundreds of vending machines in British Rail and London Underground stations. The result of three years research, the machines are made of unbreakable polycarbonate; the coin slots are unblockable; and the selection key pad is protected by a high security door frame and locking points. Holding 600 units, the machines are chilled so that the chocolates are kept in ideal conditions. A hi-tech display screen makes selections easy and the machines have change-giving facilities. These have since been upgraded by giant, free-standing machines which use CFC free refrigerants, carry the Cadbury logo and hold 800 bars of chocolate and a selection of Trebor Bassett sweets. Hi-tech display stands have also been installed in many shops; an increasing number of shop fronts have been fitted with an eye-catching Cadbury fascia; and many branded shops have been opened including at the Gatwick Airport and Dudley's Merry Hill Shopping Centre. Innovation is also evident in promotional links to such companies as British Airways and McDonalds.

The continuing growth of Cadbury in the United Kingdom is clearly dependent upon an intimate relationship between the company and its consumers. This bond has been a constant in the firm's history and will remain so as the company moves into the new millenium. Cadbury was the first major chocolate maker with its own internet web site, which has now been developed with products such as Crunchie having their own site; its Consumer Relations Department handles over 100,000 contacts annually; and in association with Save the Children, it has sponsored the Cadbury Pantomime Season. Crucially this connection with its customers has been reinforced by the opening of Cadbury World.

Since the closure of the Visitors' Department in 1970, Cadbury had received

The Chocolate credits from televisions 'Coronation Street'

annually thousands of requests for information on chocolate and Bournville and many enquiries about tours. Modern health and safety legislation precludes large-scale visits, but the company did recognise the significance of Bournville in its appeal to the public. It decided to construct a multi-million pound visitors' centre, housed mostly in a custom-built structure connected to the first floor of the old East Cocoa Block. Opening on 14 August 1990, it welcomed 400,000 people in its first year. Firmly established as one of the most popular tourist attractions in the United Kingdom, Cadbury World provides a ride, exhibition, displays and demonstrations on both the history of chocolate making and Cadbury. The whole complex exemplifies the intimate interaction of past, present and future which is evident throughout Cadbury's operations.

From its beginnings in the early 1800s, the name of Cadbury has been a positive one in the minds of British chocolate lovers. For them Cadbury means chocolate which has a unique and wonderful taste and which is top quality, but also it signifies a company which can be trusted and has principles. Increasingly Cadbury has recognised the significance of these links and gradually it has introduced advertising focusing on 'Cadburyness' as well as on individual brands. Such an approach seeks to increase the prominence of the Cadbury name and to use it as an umbrella for its diverse confectionery products. This began in 1988 when 'CDM' itself was publicised in a major new advertsing campaign using the slogan, 'Cadbury's. The Chocolate. The Taste.' The campaign used a variety of new commercials, each of which ended with the tearing open of a corner of the wrapper to reveal the Cadbury name on a chunk of 'CDM'. This concept was further developed into that of the 'Master Brand' initiative to provide a global campaign for Cadbury chocolate as opposed to the individual Cadbury brands. The initiative focused on four main icons - the Cadbury signature, the glass and a half, the colour purple and a swirl of chocolate. A new advertisement was also created which did not focus on one product, rather it uses the Cadbury logo with the image of a glass and a half of milk pouring into a swirl of chocolate and accompanied by the song 'Show Me Heaven'. To emphasise this Master Brand concept Cadbury ventured into broadcasting sponsorship in 1996 by paying to have its name associated with 'Coronation Street', one of the United Kingdom's most popular television programmes.

> *Coronation Street has earned a very special place in the hearts and minds of British TV viewers and it was important for Granada that our broadcast sponsor had a similar stature - and Cadbury fits the bill perfectly. (Andrea Wonfer, Joint Managing Director of Granada Television. 'We're streets ahead' Cadbury News April '96).*

A chocolate Coronation Street appears on the screen at the start, middle and end of each episode and features animated chocolate characters either promoting single brands or the Master Brand. Through its link up with Coronation Street, Cadbury gained five gold awards and the Grand Prix at the 1996 Institute of Sales Promotion awards.

Cadbury is a modern company, forward-looking and keen to embrace innovative technology. In 1995 Cadbury Schweppes was voted Britain's most admired company in a survey in 'Management Today' magazine. This looked at areas of business such as quality of management, financial soundness, quality of products, and services and marketing. According to Charles Skinner of the magazine, Cadbury Schweppes was outstanding in another feature. During the early 1990s it had transformed itself *'from a big business operator to a truly global operator'*. Yet as Cadbury leaps ahead it holds fast to the principles upheld by its founder, John Cadbury. His successors are determined to provide not only quality products but also to give something back to society. Significantly in 1996 the Princess Royal presented Cadbury's with a certificate honouring the company's efforts to raise funds for the charity Save the Children'

At the core of the Cadbury business is a passion for making the best chocolate with a unique taste. That passion is the key to the company's growth and to its present Master Brand approach. When John Cadbury opened his shop in 1824 he was pledged to provide quality goods. His resolve was shared by his sons, Richard and George, and it has been upheld by their descendants. As Cadbury reaches out to the new millenium, that commitment to the principles held dear by the company's founders remains as powerful a force as ever. Sir Dominic Cadbury has made plain this essential bond between the past, present and future.

> *Today we are very much an international business in terms of people, markets and brands. We look different and we are different but our commitment to the values we have inherited has not changed. These values, the skills of Cadbury Schweppes people and our famous brands will enable us to chart our future course with confidence.*

There is no doubt that the Cadbury passion for high standards has had deep effects. For many British people good chocolate is Cadbury and Cadbury's is good chocolate. Such a fine reputation is a fitting tribute to the integrity of the company's founders.

Glossary

Nibs	-	Small fragments of cocoa bean kernel which remain after breaking beans and removing the shell.
Liquor/Mass	-	a thick liquid produced when roasted cocoa nibs are ground
Refined plain chocolate	-	Smooth dark chocolate where the main ingredients are mass.
Traveller/Representative	-	Personnel employed to visit shops and stores to promote the company's products.
Melangeur	-	One of the earliest machines used to grind cocoa, sugar and milk into paste.
Milk chocolate crumb	-	A crumbly substance formed by drying a mixture of milk, sugar and mass.
Moulds	-	Hollow objects used to form bars of chocolate or shapes, like Easter eggs.
Assortments	-	A mixture of small individual chocolates in a box such as Cadbury's Milk Tray and Cadbury's Roses.
Selflines	-	Identical chocolates packed in bags or boxes.
Countlines	-	Individually wrapped chocolate covered bars sold by number rather than weight.
Refining	-	Grinding to make chocolate smoother
Snap	-	Sound and sensation of breaking chunks off a block of chocolate.
Continuous Machinery	-	Equipment where chocolate is continuously flowing into and out of the machine.
Tempering	-	The cooling and heating of chocolate in a controlled manner to produce chocolate which is smooth and glossy.